By three methods we may learn wisdom: first, by reflection, which is noblest; second, by imitation, which is easiest; and third by experience, which is the bitterest.

Confucius

First published in 2018 by Barrallier Books Pty Ltd,
trading as Echo Books. The text was updated on 10 October 2018 to reflect
some re-wording on page 85.

Registered Office: 35-37 Gordon Avenue, West Geelong, Victoria 3220,
Australia.

www.echobooks.com.au

Copyright © Peter Dunn

National Library of Australia Cataloguing-in-Publication entry.

Author: Dunn, Peter.

Title: Preparing to Lead in a Crisis.

ISBN: 9780648202585 : Paperback

A catalogue record for this book is available from the National Library of Australia

Book and cover design by Peter Gamble, Canberra.
Set in Garamond Premier Pro Display, 12/17 and Minerva Modern.

Image sources: Dreamstime and selected images by Lindy Dunn

www.echobooks.com.au

PREPARING
TO
LEAD
IN A CRISIS

PETER DUNN

 **ECHO** BOOKS

PREFACE

Preparing to Lead in a Crisis is a practical guide for the development of senior leaders or those aspiring to such positions.

The frequency of crises is increasing. This increase is due to many factors including climate change, financial mismanagement and poor political decision-making. Societies are more connected than ever before with the various forms of social media adding to the 24/7 news cycle. Unfolding crises are covered in minute detail and instantly shared. While much of this information is accurate, a lot is not and this leads to increased confusion. When a poor response occurs, senior leaders are targeted.

What areas do senior leaders need to focus on to achieve the best possible outcome? How do they prepare themselves?

After a crisis has passed and some time has elapsed to allow wounds to heal, organisations and governments frequently feel that an objective assessment of a response to a crisis can be conducted. Such assessments are not designed to assign blame or fame. Rather, they look at the facts and involve extensive interviews with key people involved in the event. After years of work identifying the causes of poor responses to crises, four themes have emerged: poor senior leadership behaviours; poor planning; failure to use information and intelligence effectively; and ineffective resource allocation.

This book examines actions that senior leaders can take to rapidly improve their expertise in these critical areas. It is designed to share knowledge and experiences that can enhance a senior leader's readiness to lead in a crisis.

Burnt bushland after the 2009 Victorian bushfire disaster.

CONTENTS

INTRODUCTION

Crises can occur at any time and in any organisation or community. At such times, leaders at all levels are tested and very few would say that, on reflection, they did not learn from such a difficult experience. Good leaders are always learning. The common challenge they face is that they are time poor. They therefore need to be selective in where they devote their energy.

What makes a good leader? A quick internet search of 'Leadership' reveals almost 800,000 hits in less than one second. The volume of leadership development programs is huge and they are diverse. Should a leader seeking to improve their capabilities focus on increasing their technical skills, their budget management acumen or their personal leadership qualities? Which programs, activities or consultancies would be best to use for their current situation? Which knowledge areas should be prioritised over others?

Over the past 15 years Noetic Solutions Pty Ltd, a strategic consulting company with offices in Australia and the USA, has been undertaking assignments to examine numerous types of disasters. They have documented the lessons that can be drawn with the benefit of hindsight and then worked with clients to ensure that these lessons are implemented and so become 'lessons learnt'.

I worked with Noetic in examining this rich data base of information on disasters to see if there were any common themes that were evident when the response to a disaster did not achieve the desired results. When a response was poor (to a part or the whole of a disaster) four specific areas emerged as being key contributors:

- **Poor Senior Leadership Skills.** When the response to a disaster was poor, ineffective leadership at the higher levels (strategic or executive levels) was often evident. This deficiency manifested itself through deficiencies in two areas of senior leadership:
  - Senior leaders who failed to recognise the development of an 'out-of-scale' event or think strategically struggled. Some were simply overwhelmed by a crisis as they did not have the techniques needed to succeed in such a situation.
  - Senior leaders who were unapproachable, prone to excessive physical overreaction (shouting, swearing, etc.) or openly pessimistic during the crisis failed to achieve the best response their organisation could achieve.
- **Poor Planning.** Poor responses were often characterised by poor planning, including pre-planning and planning that failed to adapt to a changing situation.
- **Failure to Use Information and Intelligence Effectively.** Many of the responses showed a failure to examine in-coming information, to analyse it, and to use it to predict what might happen in the future.
- **Ineffective Resource Allocation.** The ineffective allocation of resources (especially scarce resources) was also a recurring theme. This included inaction where resources were not allocated to the response because of a paralysis in decision-making at senior levels.

> If leaders are to concentrate on any areas to improve their ability to manage a crisis, priority should be given to:
> - senior leadership techniques and behaviours
> - planning
> - use of information and intelligence
> - resource allocation

Leaders should not draw the inference that they need only to study the four thematic areas that have been identified here. Broad leadership development is still required. However, if a leader needs to be particularly good in any specific areas of leadership and management, understanding these four key areas is a priority.

A person given a leadership position unexpectedly, should start with learning to master these four areas and continue to broaden their overall leadership knowledge. If a crisis emerges early in their tenure, being aware of, and prepared to avoid, these four common areas of failure provides an excellent foundation.

As we now have data that show poor responses are characterised by the presence of these four critical points of failure, then we must be able to highlight actions that can be taken to improve the skills of senior leaders to minimise the risk of future failures. This book does just that.

Sadly, there are numerous crises that could be used as a basis for this book as such events happen all too frequently. Conservatively, we should anticipate more of the same, with climate change predictions pointing to significant increases in natural disasters and greater extremes.

I have used information from each of the following disasters and operations in the preparation of this book:

- 2003 Canberra Bushfires
- 2005 South Australian Eyre Peninsular Fires
- 2006 Cyclone Larry
- 2007 Equine Influenza Outbreak
- 2009 Victorian Bushfires
- 2010 West Australian Toodyay Fires
- 2010 Deepwater Horizon Well Blowout
- 2011 Cyclone Yasi
- ADF Strategic Operations in the Iraq War
- 2011 Victorian Floods
- 2011 Montara Oil Rig Blowout

- 2011 Western Australia Margaret River Fires
- 2011 Queensland Wivenhoe Dam Operations Failure (review of Commission of Inquiry evidence and findings)
- 2014 Sydney Lindt Café Siege
- 2014 Australian Contribution to the West African Ebola Crisis Response

The data show that each disaster had its own peculiarities and challenges but the four areas of failure were common to all instances of poor response.

The fact that many of the disaster responses examined contained elements that could have been more effectively executed should not detract from the fact that many crisis responses have been very good. The senior leaders involved have demonstrated a high level of crisis management skill. The Aspen Medical response to the 2014 West African Ebola crisis is but one example of an excellent response to a crisis.

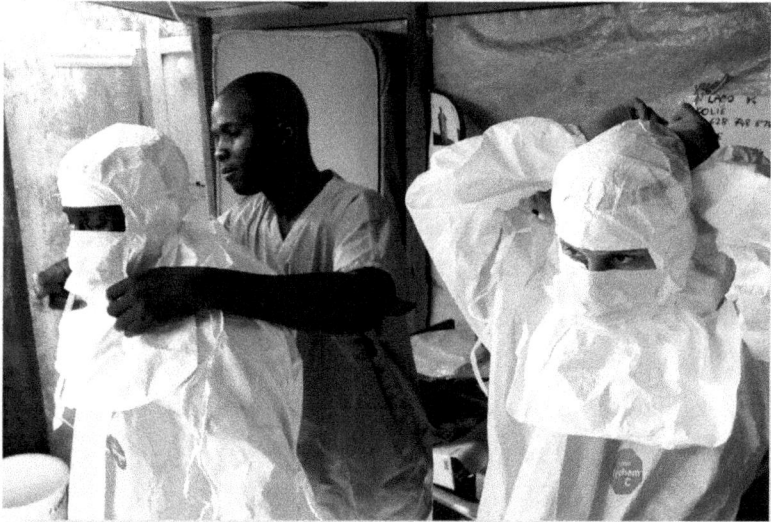

Aspen Medical West Africa Ebola Response, 2014

I have spent the last eight years running programs that specifically highlighted these common points of crisis response failure. The constant question to me has been: 'What can we do to improve ourselves and our organisations to avoid these pitfalls in the future?' Enquiries have come from private enterprise, the public sector, emergency management organisations, aid and development organisations, the health and education sectors and many other areas, including Australian and international organisations.

By using the experience gained through holding leadership positions in a diverse range of organisations and engaging with literally hundreds of people in organisations that needed to be ready to respond to a disaster, I have developed a suggested list of leadership skills or techniques that can reduce poor crisis response outcomes. Senior leaders need to employ these effectively if they are to prepare themselves to lead in a crisis.

The list will not be a perfect fit for every senior leader. However, the data show that by excelling in the areas covered in this book the chances of a successful response to a disaster will be greatly improved. Also, by developing the leadership skills discussed in the following chapters, senior leaders will be able to better manage their time between doing their daily job and learning to improve.

I have grouped the leadership skills/techniques required to lead in a crisis into three parts of this book.

- Part 1—Senior Leaders and Planning addresses the essential elements of planning on which senior leaders must focus to prepare to lead in a crisis and then to execute a successful crisis response plan.
- Part 2—Organisational Crisis Leadership Techniques introduces a number of other organisational leadership techniques that will assist a senior leader to ensure that their organisation can meet the many demands that might be placed on it.
- Part 3—Senior Leaders' Behaviour During a Crisis is focused on identifying those behaviours that every senior leader must exhibit when leading a crisis response. Part 3 draws heavily on Parts 1 and 2 as an understanding of crisis response planning and organisational leadership techniques provides the foundation for a confident senior leader who is calm, sensibly optimistic and approachable during a crisis.

This book is not intended to develop new leadership theories or to present existing theories in full. It is intended to be a practical guide. Many leaders and participants in post-disaster workshops and other learning activities have tested the suggestions and ideas I have presented here. Many are using them now.

Initially, I targeted this book at emergency management organisations tasked with the response to natural and man-made disasters. As the development of content progressed, it became increasingly apparent that the same problems are evident in the responses of a wide variety of other organisations that face crises.

Government agencies are expert in taking draft policies through a very thorough bureaucratic process to ensure that they are well formulated. Despite this, they now face many unforeseen situations that demand a crisis response. The ubiquitous social media, the 24/7 news cycle and the insatiable desire of politicians to be seen as strong and decisive leaders combine to put the bureaucratic process under enormous pressure. Policy must sometimes be formulated 'on the run' without full

Government leaders need to develop strategies to prevent policy crises developing.

consideration of possible unintended consequences. Many unintended consequences need to be mitigated urgently when they occur.

Examples of some government policy crises that have occurred in recent years in Australia are:

- 2007 Northern Territory Aboriginal Intervention
- 2014 Home Insulation Program (HIP)—'Pink Batts'
- 2016 On-Line Census failure
- 2017 National Power Crisis

Each of these events required a crisis response from government agencies. For some senior leaders, it was their first experience of formulating the urgent actions required to address a large-scale crisis.

Development of a national energy policy in Australia in 2017 required crisis management skills.

Another important product of my research has been the identification of areas that are NOT routinely being recognised as causing a poor crisis response. The following areas have not emerged as consistent causes of a poor overall response to a crisis:

- The 'technical' ability of senior leaders
- The training of individuals involved as first responders
- Equipment failures or a general lack of equipment (with the notable exception of communications equipment), and
- Budget allocations

Paradoxically, many of the actions taken by governments and organisations to better prepare for a future crisis have focused on these areas. New equipment has been purchased, first responder training improved and budgets increased. All improvements are welcome but similar improvements in senior leadership development are infrequent. Perhaps some actions are more suitable than others to publicise and demonstrate activity. Perhaps they are just easier to action than doing the things senior leaders need to prepare themselves for a better response to the next crisis.

PART 1
SENIOR LEADERS AND PLANNING

I have always found that plans are useless but planning is indispensable.

Dwight Eisenhower

CHAPTER 1
FRAMING THE EVENT

It has become clear that the expectations of communities in which major emergencies are managed has undergone significant change. The 'interconnectedness' of society has increased exponentially with the almost universal uptake of the many readily available forms of social media. Because of this rapid expansion of communications, there is a reduced public appetite for failure. Apparent failures are now highlighted in almost real time and a running commentary on the effectiveness of leaders at many levels is widely available.

Expectations have also changed because of the impact of what can be described as 'out-of-scale' events. These occur when established predictive tools are unable to manage the inputs they are receiving. These events disrupt conventional thinking based on long term experience and well-developed methodologies. This is not to say that such events have not occurred throughout history; they have. Rather, there appears to be an increasing frequency of these events and the social and economic effects of these disasters have become massive.

Framing the Event

Over the last 15 years many major disasters have so overwhelmed the planning and execution of responses that they need to be considered as out-of-scale. None of the previous response mechanisms have applied and new approaches were required. One such approach is to devote more effort to determining the exact nature of the emerging crisis, how it might develop and what the impacts might be. This is called 'framing the event'.

With the possible exception of broad area flooding, major crises develop very quickly from seemingly routine events. The response to the 2003 Canberra bushfires, the 2005 Eyre Peninsula fires and the 2011 Brisbane flood emergency (Wivenhoe Dam management) were all characterised by an initial pre-planned approach. On-ground responses followed well practised sequences with which emergency managers were familiar and comfortable. Within a very short time these routine problems turned into out-of-scale events.

Canberra bushfires 2003

The subsequent inquiries into these disasters found that many of the senior leaders involved were focused on implementing the existing pre-planned emergency responses in their areas of responsibility and did not recognise the external signals indicating that the pre-planned measures needed to be dramatically modified immediately after the initial response was made. Senior leaders had not accurately framed the events they were confronting.

> Correctly framing the event is one of the most important crisis management actions a senior leader can undertake. This will form the basis of all response activities that follow.
>
> To frame an event accurately, a senior leader must look both inside and *outside* their jurisdiction or areas of responsibility. Consideration must be given to what is going on in other areas of interest as well as in those areas for which the senior leader has direct responsibility.
>
> Once an event has been correctly framed, the *context* for a specific crisis response within the senior leader's area of responsibility can be established. Accurately framing an event, however, requires the senior leader to develop new understanding and skills such as recognising unconscious bias, working with ambiguity and the need for 'presence'.

Unconscious Bias

It would be easy to attribute an inaccurate framing of the event to the training that many managers receive. Repetitive exercises in emergency service organisations or the military, for example, are designed to ensure a rapid and predictable response to a given situation. This training can result in a 'business-as-usual' approach to emerging situations.

Some commentators have criticised emergency managers for this approach but such criticism assumes that those responsible for the initial response should have immediately grasped the magnitude of the emerging situation. This misses the point entirely. The initial responses to the many crises I studied for this book were, in almost every case, perfectly reasonable and well executed. The failure lay in the inability of senior leaders to frame the event accurately by looking more widely at the conditions developing around them.

Once the initial response was made in accordance with existing guidelines there was little examination of the implications of the myriad pieces of information that were pouring into emergency management centres. Why was this huge volume of information seemingly ignored? Response plans were not updated and amended to reflect the changes that were occurring on the ground. Unconscious biases were probably acting as brakes on the leader's ability to change and move forward.

Decision-makers often demonstrate unconscious bias by falling back on what is familiar and comfortable when are confronted with, and sometimes overwhelmed by, very large volumes of unfamiliar information. This 'avalanche' can cause leaders to make irrational and simplified decisions; irrational, that is, when hindsight is applied. Several simplifying mental actions known as 'heuristics' are always in play and senior leaders must be aware of their presence and impact on unconscious decision-making. Heuristics involve mental shortcuts that provide swift estimates about the possibility of uncertain occurrences[1]. Heuristics make it simple for the human brain to manage large volumes of unfamiliar data. This can, however, lead to the introduction of major systemic errors as leaders demonstrate unconscious bias by reverting to what they know and understand.

When a disaster is emerging, speed of response is of the essence. This applies in an emerging financial management crisis, a blowout on an oilrig, a pandemic, a government policy failure or a bushfire or flood. Subordinates look to their leaders for decisive actions and directions that will allow them to respond to the emerging situation effectively. The leaders, however, are often as unprepared as their teams to deal with an unfolding and unfamiliar situation.

Leaders naturally try to simplify the mass of data with which they are presented just to make it manageable. Mental shortcuts are taken as part of this process. This is an unconscious response that all leaders experience. The attempt to simplify masses of data plus the repetitive training in initial response methods to routine incidents can drive leaders to a rapid, but rigid, approach.

---

1   Baumeister & Bushman, *Social Psychology and Human Nature*, 2nd Edition, 2010, p. 141

The effect of unconscious bias on groups also needs to be considered when trying to understand how events are framed in crises. Decisions made by a group are comforting. There is reinforcement that consensus has been reached and a response initiated. There is little comfort in making decisions as an individual. But what if the unconscious biases at work serve to create a situation which collectively simplifies the mass of information being assessed by senior leadership groups? Group decision-making can reinforce a business-as-usual response as reasonable, indeed appropriate. Accurately framing the event can become very difficult.

Senior leaders will never know when their unconscious biases are at work. After all, these biases are unconscious. In the face of a crisis we do know that heuristics will tend to cause the sorting of masses of information into simpler and more manageable packages. In a group situation, this action is happening to everyone and there is comfort being gained from being a part of that group. It is therefore quite possible that in trying to be rational about an emerging and unfamiliar situation, the collective simplification of the data leads to the group agreeing that a simple response is all that is required. Senior leaders will not be able to stop this process occurring. What is essential is for senior leaders to be keenly aware that the effect of heuristics underlies all decisions being made by the group (and by individuals) and that it cannot be stopped. Awareness of the process should enable decision-makers to avoid being seduced into over simplifying their view of unfolding events by 'groupthink' and so should lead to a more accurate framing of an event and then decisive action.

Dealing with Ambiguity

To frame an event properly, the senior leader must develop the skills to deal with ambiguity. Crises seldom appear in a structured way from a given set of pre-conditions. In the period leading to the emergence of a crisis there are nearly always warning signals of some kind. The problem is that these signals are very weak and often conflicting. Some senior leaders are comfortable operating in such an environment but most are not.

Senior leaders must be able to pick up these weak signals and then to make sense of them if they are to lead their organisation effectively in a crisis. People who understand the existence of their own unconscious biases are far better prepared mentally to open their minds to a broader range of signals. The mere fact that they know it is perfectly natural for them to seek simplification of the myriad data inputs provides them with a platform from which they can challenge their own version of the events they are witnessing. Actively challenging their own opinions or views requires courage and determination.

Courage is needed because the senior leader must be prepared to accept that despite their position and previous experiences they may, on this occasion, be quite wrong. Courage is also required for the senior leader to expose these thoughts to others in the leadership team. The days of the heroic and omnipotent leader have long gone. The effective senior leader needs to be prepared to admit that they possess their own unconscious biases and to discuss this with other members of their team. The effective senior leader needs to listen to what the other team members say while noting that all of those involved will have their own unconscious biases hard at work.

Determination is needed because challenging their own biases and those of others requires large amounts of mental effort. This determination needs to be shared by the entire senior leadership team. A strong team is essential if the weak and conflicting signals that are associated with ambiguous situations are to be identified and dissected effectively. Pooling the weak signals being received by different people greatly assists with the management of an ambiguous situation. Encouraging others to draw alternate conclusions from the weak signals they are receiving, rather than just relying on years of previous experience to construct a familiar picture of the situation, is not easy.

The knowledge gained in the planning process is a major asset in attempting to deal with ambiguity. The 'what if' questioning process described in Chapter 3—The Crisis Response Planning Process—

allows senior leaders to be more aware of what early signals indicate a developing deterioration in the situation that they are managing. Weak signals that may simply be considered as irrelevant can suddenly become extremely important if they can be seen as an indicator of one or more of the scenarios that have already been considered during the senior leader's planning process.

Collaboration also assists senior leaders deal with ambiguity. Weak, seemingly unrelated and conflicting signals that are received and possibly ignored by one organisation may make perfect sense to another organisation used to dealing with such information. If active collaboration has been established between organisations beforehand, this information can be rapidly transferred and acted upon thereby reducing the level of ambiguity that is being experienced.

Combining the outputs of the crisis response planning process with the knowledge gained from internal and external collaboration, will reduce the ambiguity of the environment in which senior leaders must work. Understanding the existence of unconscious biases enables senior leaders to sensibly challenge advice and opinions that emerge during the development of a crisis and seek more information. Full clarity will never be achieved but the level of ambiguity can be reduced by these actions.

Listening to your Critics

A simple but effective preparatory way for a senior leader to improve their ability to frame an event is to listen to what critics say about the leader's decisions and actions during routine and major responses. There are always commentators ready to criticise and this can be a source of frustration and irritation. Nevertheless, there is often an element of truth in many criticisms and they should at least be listened to.

Such criticism or commentary is another input that can help minimise unconscious bias. Taking the time to analyse the comments and to re-examine a response that has been criticised is a very good use of a senior leader's time. There are, of course, serial critics that can be very rude and, if they have a 'political ear', can create a lot of additional work by causing politicians to ask irrelevant questions on their behalf. Providing curt responses usually does not benefit anyone. Ignoring the comments or providing a rude response simply brings more criticism.

A much more useful process is to engage directly with the critic when it is both possible and reasonable to do so. It will not be possible to engage directly every time a criticism is levelled at the senior leader or their organisation. Work load will preclude that. It is possible, though, to plan and set up meetings with critics in advance at intervals that make use of quieter times. It is unlikely that the senior leader will be able to keep all of these meetings but two or three each calendar year is usually enough to build an understanding of the point of view of the critic. This knowledge can be of great assistance in framing an event in the future.

Accessibility and Presence

In many of the disasters researched in the writing of this book, senior leaders have been criticised for not being accessible to their subordinates at critical, early stages of a developing disaster. This prevents their involvement in framing the event accurately with their staff. In every case examined the leaders have been people of good character with a track record of encouraging staff to use their initiative.

- In the immediate aftermath of the 2003 Canberra Bushfire disaster the then Australian Capital Territory (ACT) Chief Minister was criticised by the media and other commentators for being 'unavailable' to his emergency services operations staff and senior ACT bureaucrats on the night before the fires struck Canberra.

- After the disastrous Victorian bushfires in 2009, the Chief Police Commissioner was criticised in the media for keeping a hairdresser's appointment and later attending dinner at a restaurant in Melbourne while the disaster was emerging.

- In Western Australia in 2011, the Commissioner of Police was similarly criticised for attending a cricket match in Perth when what became a bushfire disaster was emerging in a rural area in Western Australia.

- In December 2014, a terrorist took 18 hostages in the Lindt Café in Martin Place in the Sydney CBD. The siege lasted for 17 hours and ended with two hostages killed and the terrorist dead. The NSW Police Commissioner and a Deputy Commissioner were criticised by the media during the inquest into the siege for not being more directly involved in the rescue operation. A text message sent by the Commissioner to his Deputy which ended with an apparently light-hearted comment was used as evidence to suggest a 'detached' position to the operation.

The criticism levelled at these and other senior leaders during emerging disasters was fierce. They were given no real opportunity to explain the confidence they had in their senior leadership teams and the systems that had already been established in their organisations to deal with such crises. Their reputations were dented.

This perceived lack of involvement in the early stages of the response operations meant that the leaders were required to expend considerable energy addressing criticisms of their personal performance when all of their energy should have been given to framing the event and leading the escalating response. They should also have been initiating preparations for the major recovery operations that were going to be required in their respective jurisdictions.

Obviously, senior leaders cannot be present in their organisations 24 hours a day, 7 days a week (24/7). This is discussed later in this book in relation to determining sources of qualified staff to undertake long term crisis response and then recovery operations. Senior leaders do, however, have to expect a hostile media reaction to any perceived lack of focus on their job. Such reputational damage is, in almost every case, unwarranted but it occurs.

It is unlikely that a senior leader in a highly visible position will be able to escape such attention when the media do not want to understand the need for senior leaders to delegate to others in their absence. Likewise, when they delegate in order to train subordinates to fill their role when they are unavailable, for example, because of leave, illness, accident or a personal/family crisis.

This is surprising as it seems to be accepted that even Prime Ministers and Presidents take leave for various reasons and their deputies step up and into their positions temporarily. If it is reasonable for such deputising to occur at the highest level, it should be reasonable at other levels as well, provided that the senior leader can be contacted.

In the public sector, additional pressures can arise when political leaders insist that a particular individual leader be present at all times. Senior leaders concern themselves with succession planning and therefore understand the need for the training of senior staff to step in and deputise when required. If a political leader ignores this aspect of developing a strong leadership team with depth, they weaken the overall organisation they are trying to promote. Additionally, when the time comes to replace a retiring senior leader they will have, by their own actions, narrowed the field of candidates considerably. Frequently, this narrowing occurs to the extent that no internal candidates are available for consideration for promotion at all.

Notwithstanding the above, a senior leader who has properly delegated their duties for a temporary period must now remain accessible to their organisation. They may not be physically present but their delegate must be able to reach out to them at any time should a crisis emerge, particularly to discuss the framing of the event that might be unfolding. The senior leader must then decide whether to commence the process of an early return to work or not.

Senior leaders need to know how and when they should intervene in a crisis so that they are always available to their staff and so that they may genuinely be seen by the community as leading a major response effort. This needs to be conducted in a manner that does not suggest that they do not have confidence in their staff and wish to 'micro-manage' the response.

The senior leader is leading a team. There is no way a senior leader can be across all the details of an emerging disaster and the response(s) that may be occurring. At different times during the initiation or conduct of a response to a disaster, operations teams and other officials will need to discuss possible options and consequences with their senior leaders. These discussions need to occur quickly and cannot wait until a senior leader has become 'available'. Hence, the senior leader needs to be accessible to their staff always to fulfil their role in framing the event.

This does not mean that that every small detail of a response needs to be raised with the senior leader. Intermediate leaders must also play their role in making themselves available to their subordinates and ensuring that decisions appropriate to their level are made expeditiously.

The senior leader must ensure that staff are trained and capable of fulfilling their roles. The senior leader must take steps before any emergency arises to satisfy themselves that they can be confident in the capabilities of their subordinates. This means rehearsing responses to hypothetical scenarios and debriefing subordinates on their performance in these learning situations. Also, it means that senior leaders must look closely at the level of professional training that subordinates have undertaken and be totally satisfied that all their subordinates are qualified for their role. If these pre-requisites are met and the senior leader is accessible during an emerging crisis, then the basis for effectively implementing operational response plans exists.

The best way for a senior leader to ensure that they are accessible is to maintain a presence with their staff. Regular visits to staff, attending both scheduled and impromptu briefings and travelling to visit staff providing an operational response will all ensure that the senior leader gives the necessary support to their subordinates. This support engenders confidence among staff and external stakeholders and definitely helps the senior leader to better frame the event they are confronting.

Strangely, these common-sense actions do not always occur. Some senior leaders feel that if they visit staff working areas they are somehow intruding on their subordinates or their presence will be taken as an expression of lack of confidence. The lessons learnt from disasters that have been examined indicate the opposite is true. Staff welcome frequent interactions with their senior leaders and routinely use such opportunities to 'sound out' ideas and concepts with the senior leader in an informal way.

Of course, the senior leader has experience to offer others in their organisation and this should be delivered as a key part of the training of their staff prior to a crisis emerging. However, if the senior leader is exercising presence and on each occasion, uses the time to tell subordinates how they used to do similar tasks, the staff will quickly come to resent such visits. Senior leaders must avoid this temptation.

The benefits of these interactions are reciprocal. Meeting regularly with staff allows the senior leader to readily gauge how they are coping with an emerging disaster. Subordinates who are normally extrovert who suddenly appear inwardly focused and despondent may indicate that an emerging problem is beyond the capability of the individual. This then signals to the senior leader that an area may need to be reinforced or an individual might need to be supported in some way.

Allowing staff to 'sound out' options and discuss possible consequences is very valuable for the senior leader. Ideas and concerns that otherwise may not be apparent to the senior leader can emerge. Consequences of seemingly routine actions may be much larger than the subordinate staff members have anticipated and therefore the senior leader can manage issues immediately. The senior leader can also manage expectations if they are using 'presence' in this way.

These inputs allow the senior leader to better frame the event and anticipate the future needs of their organisation. Anticipation is one of the key requirements of a successful senior leader in managing a crisis and being well informed is a key aspect of this success. Staff inputs can also serve to indicate the need for collaboration with other organisations as the senior leader is exposed to suggestions where, by engagement with other senior leaders, they can improve the response or recovery actions that are being undertaken by involving others.

When not actually interacting with staff, the senior leader still needs to remain accessible. This can be achieved through the many communication media that are routinely available to senior leaders today. What is important is how these media are managed if the senior leader is to be allowed to do their job without unnecessary interruptions.

Some senior leaders opt for using a trusted and experienced staff member as their 'chief of staff'. This person coordinates the staff's contact with the senior leader and facilitates the smooth flow of information to the senior leader. This is an increasingly common mode of operations for senior leaders today. Sadly, many senior leaders do not fully understand the real role of a chief of staff and routinely misuse this position.

The origins of the position of chief of staff are usually traced back to military organisations. Historically, the military (particularly large army organisations) used the chief of staff to ensure the efficient functioning of a large headquarters by properly coordinating all staff actions. The military chief of staff was not authorised to be a filter for information reaching the commander of the organisation. They were a coordinator. Recent political history in Australia is replete with examples of ministerial chiefs of staff controlling access to ministers and prime ministers and supposedly speaking with the authority of their superior. It is hardly surprising that these actions were divisive and even corrosive within government circles.

Senior leaders in large organisations can derive enormous value from establishing a position of chief of staff in their offices but they need to understand exactly what the role they are creating is intended to do and how the new position should be used to facilitate a more efficient organisation. They clearly need to understand the risks inherent in operating this way.

> The position of a chief of staff should never be created to control access to the senior leader either of key subordinates or of information. The role should be to coordinate.

A better way to ensure that a senior leader is not constantly interrupted by trivia or those enthusiastic subordinates wanting 'face time with the boss' is the establishment of simple staff protocols relating to access. These might be a statement describing the levels of incident that are to be brought to the attention of the senior leader and when they are to be raised. For example, routine incidents might be reported in a weekly summary to the senior leader. Major incidents might (and usually would) trigger an immediate report to the senior leader. An escalating major incident or a critical incident might trigger an immediate assembly of the senior leader's key subordinates in a face-to-face briefing and decision-making session.

The senior leader's key subordinates should be held responsible and accountable for the efficient operation of this or any like system of access. If a chief of staff is appointed, they should assist the key subordinates in the coordination of such a system. But it is emphasised that it is the key subordinates that hold the accountability for the effectiveness of the system.

The senior leader does not have the privilege of turning their mobile phone off unless there is another guaranteed form of communication that can be used to contact them quickly. Office doors cannot be shut and key subordinates ignored. Senior leadership positions require 24/7 availability and this must be managed carefully if the senior leader is to survive.

Following the suggested ways of ensuring accessibility and presence gives the senior leader a better ability to frame the event unfolding before them. They are then able to determine when and how they should intervene as the crisis is developing.

Clear understanding of protocols surrounding access and presence makes the senior leader more effective in collaborating with other like organisations and in providing an organisational umbrella to prevent unnecessary distractions from penetrating. The senior leader will be able to lead, confident in the knowledge that the response occurring is the best that can be provided by the organisation and that the nature of the crisis they are facing is better understood. Needs will be anticipated and resources gathered and deployed in an efficient way. The crisis may not be averted but a credible leadership pattern will be evident as an accurately framed event unfolds.

Strategy
A plan of action designed to achieve a long-term or overall objective
Collins Dictionary

Chapter 2
Thinking Strategically

There are at least two applications of the term 'strategy' that can be used by senior leaders. Firstly, there is the temporal aspect of looking to the long term and making plans relating to the future state of their organisation. Senior leaders can define a future state in terms of goals or objectives and a path can be mapped out to allow an organisation to achieve them. This process depends on making assumptions based on information that is known at the time. This is pre-planning and this is essential when numerous elements need to be able to respond to an event in a coordinated manner.

Secondly, strategy relates to achieving an immediate objective. This element of the definition requires overarching strategies to be considered when quickly producing a plan of action to respond to an emerging crisis. This especially relates to planning the response to an unforeseen crisis. As the response commences, senior leaders must ensure that 'big picture' and long term issues are not lost in the midst of the frenetic activity that is associated with a crisis response.

Frequently, senior leaders take one or other of these two elements of the definition of strategy and focus their role on working in that selected sphere. For example, some senior leaders invest heavily in defining goals or objectives and rigidly adhere to these. Others feel that such an investment of their time is wasteful and reduces their flexibility to respond to changing circumstances. Such actions can produce a skewed perspective of where the senior leader's attention should be directed. It is essential that senior leaders address both aspects of strategy within their organisations.

When framing an event that is emerging, senior leaders need to constantly think at the strategic level and maintain situational awareness.

Strategic Actions

Strategic actions are those that have a *long term* and *large impact* on a diverse range of connected people and activities. Strategic actions may be undertaken by staff who are not in senior leadership positions. On occasions, a decision taken by a low or mid-level person can have far reaching consequences. Therefore, while it is common to assign the strategic thinking role to a senior leader, those leaders must also consider what decisions might be taken within their organisation that could bring serious, unintended consequences.

Actions taken by emergency management personnel deployed in response to a major bushfire can provide examples of strategic actions that produce undesired and unintended consequences. For example, if an incident controller on a fire ground gave a direction to use heavy earthmoving equipment to construct a firebreak in a specific geographic area, it is possible that some irreversible damage might be done to an environmentally sensitive zone that could affect water catchments and/or biodiversity for years to come.

Similarly, policy decisions by government agencies might produce unintended consequences in the long term and cause the government of the day great concern. Such poor policy decisions may generate the need to urgently modify policy settings in a portfolio area with potentially quite severe consequences for individual constituents and the government itself.

The situations above highlight the need for the senior leader to set clear limits on the actions that can be taken by teams or individuals without reference back to the senior leader. Of course, the overall objective that the leader is trying to achieve in any given context must be the starting point of any consideration of the development of boundaries.

The leader needs to establish boundaries so that teams and individuals can get on with their work during a crisis and not feel that they must check everything with their leader. The boundaries should be as broad as possible (but not so broad as to allow unintended consequences to develop from actions taken at various levels within the organisation) and consistent with the leader's aim for the organisation.

This is the essence of strategic thinking. An effective leader must look at the functions of the organisation and take the time to think through the consequences of the actions that might be taken during a crisis.

By repeatedly asking the question: What could happen if x was undertaken? the leader can begin to develop a good idea of where boundaries need to be placed or where more information needs to be acquired.

For the leader to undertake the key task of strategic thinking they must first create space to take a broad and long-term views of actions and think about consequences. Time is a finite element so if the senior leader is to create space to allow time for thinking or consulting about strategic matters something has to be moved out of their schedule to accommodate the new task. Leadership positions are demanding. The leader's day (and often night) is filled with meetings, briefings, budget discussions, personnel issues, emails and communication activities. Time is the leader's most valuable commodity.

The senior leader must use risk management as a tool to create the space for strategic thinking if they are to be prepared to manage a crisis. Many senior leaders have their time consumed managing the highly probable risks that have low level consequences. The effective senior leader instead needs to be considering those less likely risks that have high or even catastrophic consequences should they be realised and become events.

Is it reasonable for the leader to simply say that their door is closed for two hours each day to allow them to have time to think strategically? Some senior leaders try this method but in almost every case they give up in sheer frustration after a few weeks. There are simply too many day to day, time critical decisions that must be made by a senior leader for this technique to be universally adopted.

An effective leader can, however, utilise the many skills that can be found in nearly all organisations to create the 'headspace' they need to open time for strategic thinking. Promising staff members can be delegated some tasks normally undertaken by the leader for a specific period. These delegations can be rotated as a part of a planned leadership development activity. Teams can be formed to consider the consequences of specific threats/hazards that are selected by the senior leader. Time can be scheduled for leadership group seminars to consider the consequences of certain actions or the lack of action in certain areas.

Leaders will be able to think of ways in which they can free up the headspace necessary to allow strategic thinking to occur in their organisation. Each will be different but one thing should remain constant: the leader's strategic thinking will involve other people in a variety of ways. Shutting the office door is not really an option.

Situational Awareness

Gaining and maintaining situational awareness is one way of ensuring flexibility in crisis responses. Developing situational awareness requires the senior leader to understand exactly what is happening 'on the ground'. Information must be passed to the senior leader in a timely and organised way. The flow should be rapid but staff on the ground should not be overburdened with requests from senior leaders for more and more information.

Subordinates need to understand, through the training they are given, that information requirements can change and so variations to the planned reporting process may be required. It is the senior leader's responsibility to ensure that staff understand that the nature and amount of support provided to them will depend, in large measure, on the situational awareness that can be maintained by their senior leaders. If a senior leader is to anticipate the needs of subordinates, they need to understand the situation that is being faced by those subordinates.

In some of the crises that have been examined there is evidence of crisis response personnel either withholding or ignoring key elements of information in the situation reports they submitted to senior leaders. Some response personnel expressed frustration at the requirement to provide regular situation reports to their senior leaders. Sometimes they felt that they were too busy to provide the reports. At other times, they were reluctant to report failures and tried to fix errors or failings before they were reported to their senior leaders. These circumstances contributed to a low level of situational awareness at the senior leadership level.

Senior leaders must be prepared to physically observe the actual situation that is developing for themselves. If it is understood that the senior leader is very likely to make short visits to dispersed organisational personnel there will be a much more regular information flow.

Evidence was also found of senior leaders being unreasonable and inflexible in their demands for information from their subordinates. Senior leaders who were unused to dealing with ambiguity and who were unable to detect weak signals often fell into this category.

Many senior leaders fail to use a variety of information sources when they are trying to build up their situational awareness. A key aspect of trying to achieve an overall objective is to be alert to what is happening in other related areas. A 'tunnel vision' approach that sees the senior leader fixate only on the information that is flowing upwards in their organisation will probably mean that they will miss important pieces of information that are well known in other related organisations. This means that senior leaders must be able to lift themselves up and out of the response data and observe what information is circulating in other organisations and from other sources.

Media sources of Situational Awareness

Social media, television and radio provide a large amount of information that contributes to a senior leader's situational awareness. Some senior leaders have adapted to this change and employed a variety of media forms during a crisis to receive and disseminate information to communities, shareholders and many other stakeholders. However, the rate of increase in the use of social media has been exponential and some senior leaders have had difficulty adjusting to a new set of rules and conventions that need to be observed when using these sources.

Senior leaders need people who are skilled in the use of all forms of media to manage the receipt and dissemination of information that is available during a crisis. If the senior leader does not build this capacity in their organisation they will be overwhelmed. The aim of this management should be to use a variety of media forms to receive and disseminate information and to monitor sources of information to understand what is being circulated by reporters (professionals or community members and other stakeholders). Information that originates from near the heart of a crisis can significantly add to the senior leader's situational awareness. This is discussed further in Chapter 7—Developing Intelligence.

Reading the Team

A large amount of situational awareness information can be gained by learning to 'read the team'. This means that a senior leader can walk into an area that is responding to an emerging crisis and, by observation, gauge whether the team is coping with the situation they are confronting or not. The senior leader must prepare for this activity as it is too late to begin such a process after a crisis has emerged.

Firstly, the senior leader must be comfortable with stepping out of their office and walking around their organisation—the 'shop floor' as it is often referred to. It may sound a little surprising, but there are more senior leaders who are quite literally scared to walk out of their office and engage directly with their staff than would be expected. I have been engaged in

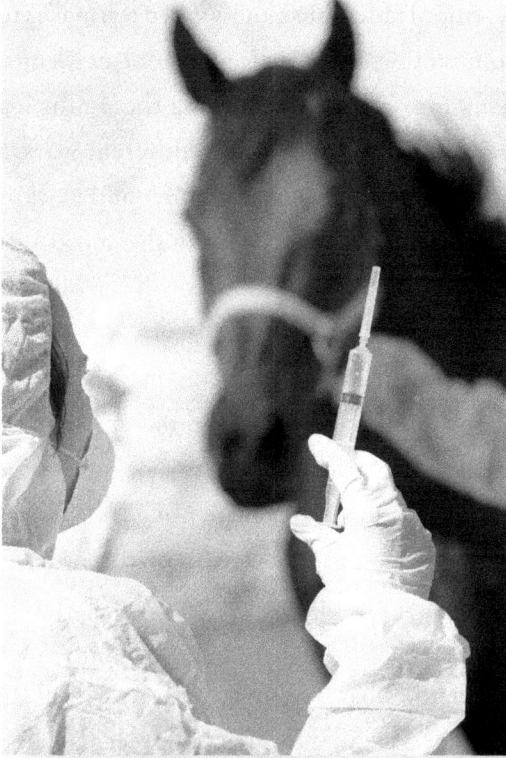

Veterinarian working to contain equine influenza.

numerous executive coaching assignments that involved the building of a senior leader's self-confidence to allow them to be comfortable when walking around their organisation and directly engaging with their teams. This element of confidence is a 'must have' for senior leaders.

In many of the crises examined for this book, various senior leaders were not fully engaged with their teams. This appears to be more prevalent when there are strong technical qualifications required for the senior leadership position. When technical requirements are emphasised over inclusive leadership requirements in selecting senior leaders, a future risk is generated and this must be mitigated. This aspect of the senior leader's role in leading in a time of crisis is covered more fully in Part 3—Senior Leaders' Behaviour During a Crisis.

Secondly, a senior leader must know what 'normal' is for their team(s). Assume for a moment that all senior leaders routinely engage directly with their staff. As they move from area to area the senior leader will notice how different sections or groups work in different ways. Some areas will be quiet and purposeful; others will be louder and working on issues as a team or in small groups. Large variations in the approach to work will be observed. The 'volume' will be different as will the observable 'happiness' of various teams.

Even though there will be large variations in the approach to conducting work these signals will represent the normal way an organisation goes about the routine tasks required. Discerning the normal must be undertaken over a period, as the variations in approach are not always clear. Work methods will only come together to give a picture of the normal over time and therefore the senior leader must make visiting the 'shop floor' a regular and directed activity. The senior leader should not simply want to be seen but rather should be gauging what is normal.

When a crisis emerges, an informed senior leader can build situational awareness further by watching how the various sections of staff are going about their now rapidly increasing amount of work and moving from normal work levels into overdrive. Loud and energetic areas might become very quiet—are they being overwhelmed by the emerging crisis? Previously quiet and purposeful areas might now be marked by staff using loud, directive instructions—are they taking direct control of a life-threatening situation? A pall of unhappiness might descend on a previously very happy area. These changes from the normal are extremely valuable additions to the senior leader's situational awareness and the leader needs to actively seek these additional inputs.

The 2 Up and 2 Down Principle

Clearly, there are not enough hours in a day to allow the senior leader to move around their organisation and engage with every individual present. The *2 Up and 2 Down Principle* is an excellent tool for senior leaders developing their organisational engagement plan (yes—it should be a 'plan'). Using this principle, the senior leader should seek out and engage staff that are one and two levels below them in the organisation, usually starting with the second level down. Similarly, the senior leader should be free to engage with superiors who are one and two levels above them in the organisation.

Using the *2 Up 2 Down Principle* is also a way of reducing the impact of the unconscious biases held by others and of reducing the filtering effect that occurs naturally in organisational hierarchies. These extra layers of information help to build the senior leader's situational awareness.

Reaching up two levels provides the most senior level leader the same opportunity. The senior leader who reaches up directly to perhaps board members or government ministers gains the additional benefit of a clear insight into the most senior level leader's intentions. Clear understanding of the most senior leader's intentions is a critical requirement for a successful response to an emerging crisis by subordinate leaders.

Take a moment to think about your own organisation. As a senior leader are you free to move around and engage 2 Up and 2 Down? The answer from many readers will be an emphatic No! Rigid organisations frown on or even forbid this type of interaction. All information in these organisations is passed from one level to the next with no overlapping of the style required to operate 2 Up and 2 Down. Intermediate levels of leadership often fret about what is being said by their staff in their absence or they worry that a subordinate leader might outshine them when they are engaging with their immediate superior.

These are very real and common organisational matters and the effective senior leader needs to find ways of overcoming such restrictions. A small confidence building step is to initiate a protocol that requires senior leaders employing the *2 Up 2 Down Principle* to speak with the intermediate leader to back-brief them on the engagement that has just occurred. This guarantees that surprises will be avoided and confidence will grow.

But it is stressed that this is a process that requires a lot of effort to introduce. The results, however, will speak for themselves and overall situational awareness will be improved.

Regular face-to-face contact 2 down allows the senior leader to perform one of their most important roles—*removing barriers to effective staff performance*. Hidden barriers to performance can often be exposed by asking the simple question: Is there anything stopping you from doing your best that I can assist you in overcoming? This conversation takes the senior leader into a critical element of their role and one that is truly appreciated by their staff. Rather than 'micro-managing' the senior leader can bring their organisational power to support the efforts of their team.

The senior leader is the person who can redistribute resources quickly and is usually authorised to seek additional resources from external organisations. The senior leader is also able to bring experience to bear on helping a team solve a problem quickly. Making themselves accessible for this role is an essential requirement for success. Instead of giving orders regarding matters of detail and execution, the senior leader can shift to a manner that has them asking teams what they need by way of assistance to complete the tasks they are tackling. In a crisis, this sense of team is very powerful. It also continues to add to the situational awareness of senior leaders as they experience true engagement with their people and those people become truly engaged with the organisation.

Many senior leaders find it difficult to work in this way. All too often they see themselves as sitting at the apex of their organisation and see directions and responses moving vertically up and down from their executive position. A change in mindset is required that links distributed leadership processes (see Chapter 5—Distributed Leadership) with a coaching or facilitating role for the leader. Senior leaders can be truly effective at removing barriers if they have a picture of their position being one that is out to one side of their organisation, able to move 2 up and 2 down and facilitate actions to solve the myriad problems a crisis presents.

This activity does not replace the traditional leadership chain; rather it supplements it. Daily interactions still need to occur within the designated organisational structure. Senior leaders should, however, venture out of their 'comfort zone' and engage with different levels in their organisation on a regular basis. Once this engagement becomes common practice, organisational teams and the most senior leaders should recognise the benefits that this system brings in terms of allowing the senior leaders to build improved situational awareness and to allow them to remove barriers that are preventing people from reaching their full potential.

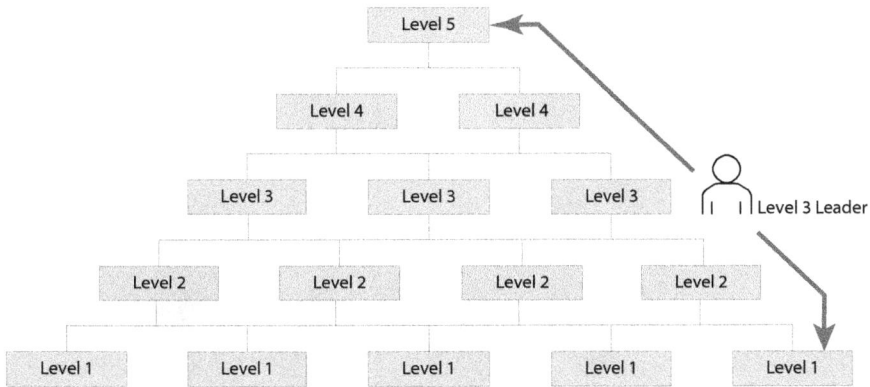

2 Up 2 Down Leadership

Chapter 3
The Crisis Response
Planning Process

When an emerging event has been accurately framed and the responsible senior leaders are thinking strategically with the input of high levels of situational awareness, they are ready to begin the detailed crisis response planning process.

All organisations routinely use planning skills. Government departments develop business plans to progress policy initiatives, emergency management agencies make plans to manage new hazards that appear in their jurisdictions, financial institutions plan to adjust to altered financial regulation and transparency requirements. Corporations plan actions to increase shareholder wealth and families plan to buy major items such as a house or car. All activities require some planning and there are many planners who manage day to day planning requirements very well.

If you agree with these statements you could be forgiven for wondering why the next two chapters of this book are devoted to planning. One of the major problems identified in the research generating this book was that when a poor response to a crisis occurred, poor planning was evident. This was demonstrated by the observed inability of some senior leaders to vary plans when unexpected conditions were encountered.

Pre-planned, routine responses are applied in contexts that require much, much more than that. The planning for routine responses is well honed but that is often where the response planning stops. More assets are applied doing the same as before with predictably poor results. Planning for a crisis response requires a much more detailed and educational approach and needs to be formalised to ensure nothing is left out of consideration of the emerging crisis. Being prepared for an out-of-scale event is not multiplying the routine response by a factor of, say, 10!

The strength of a plan derives not so much from the initial plan that is developed but rather the flexibility that the planning process provides. The military adage that 'even the best plans do not survive after the first shot is fired' is applicable to a very wide variety of plans. To doggedly stick to the letter of the original plan invites failure. However, using the knowledge that has been developed during the planning process to modify a response gives an opportunity to achieve success.

Planning is not an art; there are sound methodologies that can and should be used to ensure that the plan prepared is:

- robust and based on clear, logical thinking
- the outcome of an analytical process and not someone's best guess
- an educational process for the senior leader and key members of the organisational team.

One of the most effective methods that can be used to develop even the most complex plan is the *assessment process*. Like the distributed leadership system covered in Chapter 5, it may have its origins in military organisations but it has since been used by different organisations to help develop their planning capabilities over many years. As is the way with these adoptions they are usually accompanied with rebadging and customisation. Frequently this customisation leads to a dilution of the original strength of the process so great care must be taken to understand just what this process is actually about before changes are made.

The Assessment Process

The assessment process begins with framing the event (see Chapter 1— Framing the Event) to understand the context of the specific situation with which the senior leader is confronted. Senior leaders initially need to look at the wider implications of the emerging event before narrowing their focus to their areas of responsibility. This wider examination allows the context of the specific challenge being faced to be clearly understood.

Logical deductions are made from factors that emerge from a study of the context and other directions that may be applicable (for example, time or budget limitations). This process leads methodically to a series of viable options for action that are open to planners to consider and finally to the selection of the best option to be taken. A detailed plan can then be developed to pursue this option.

It is a process that may be used in a short form or a very detailed and thoroughly documented form. Once the senior leader fully understands the context of the crisis they are confronting they are then able to quickly produce a plan that is well informed and that retains full flexibility to allow it to be changed as the crisis evolves.

Relief supplies being delivered in Christchurch after the 2011 earthquake.

The Context

Accurately framing the event is the most important element in establishing the *context* within which the crisis response plan is to be produced. This may seem obvious but senior leaders who believe that they have a firm grip on what is going on around them often leave out this critical step. Gathering a small group of trained planners together to frame the event accurately and review the context is an essential leadership technique.

The context analysis needs to be undertaken with as many information inputs as can be harnessed in the time available. A diverse group of planners is best as they may all have different perspectives (and unconscious biases) on the crisis being faced. Building this situational awareness from a variety of inputs makes a significant difference to the outcome and needs to be stressed.

In an emerging crisis, the review of the current context should, where possible, be recorded, even if only in note form. This review will form the basis of subsequent plans and is very important as it can provide useful information to subsequent reviews of the operational response to the crisis. When the response to the crisis is considered in retrospect, there will almost certainly be different views on the relative importance of different elements of the context. This is the 'wisdom of hindsight' and needs to be balanced with a summary of just what a group of competent planners assessed as the situation *as it emerged*. The differences can be significant.

The Objective

After establishing the context it is essential that the *objective* of the efforts that are to follow is determined. Everything that follows in the assessment process will be affected by the objective that is selected.

Regardless of the circumstances of the crisis the objective of the response must be stated concisely. If this is done, then all planners will be focused on what is to be achieved and there will be a single purpose behind the remainder of the assessment process.

In situations where human lives are threatened the primary objective will always be to save those lives. In other emerging crises there can be a choice between several different objectives. In a government crisis policy making setting the objective might be to reduce existing costs or provide superior services depending on the directions given from the relevant minister. In this scenario, there will often be conflicting requirements given; for example: 'provide superior services while simultaneously reducing costs'. Regardless, a clear objective must be determined.

Factors Influencing the Objective and Limitations

In this next step of the assessment process effort is directed to *identify everything that might affect the successful achievement of the objective* that has been selected. Again, working with a small but diverse group of planners is the ideal way to proceed along this path.

To illustrate this element of the process some hypothetical examples will be used. Consider an emerging bushfire crisis first.

If several population centres are potentially under threat of fire then the objective will, of course, be to save lives. The factors that affect how this might be achieved are likely to be many. Examples could be:

- the speed at which the fire front is advancing towards population centres
- the number and usability of evacuation routes out of the affected areas
- the availability of transport to assist any people that might require evacuation
- the resources available to response agencies to stop or divert the fires before they pose a direct threat to the population centres
- weather forecasts
- the estimated numbers of people that are threatened
- the amount of fire fuel that is in the path of the fires heading to the population centres.

A second example might be the introduction of a new, urgent government policy to prevent a major budgetary crisis from materialising in a set of government provided services. Factors or limitations that may be relevant could be the:

- projected impact of ceasing some or all the services provided on those who are using the services
- cost of alternative government service delivery options
- availability of non-government means of people obtaining the services and the cost of those services
- political risk of shutting down or reducing the services in question
- money that will be saved by shutting down the services in question versus the size of the portfolio budgetary problem
- accuracy of data capture on current service use.

Deductions

Once the planning team has exhausted its efforts in producing the list of factors that might affect the objective, it is time to examine the effect that each of these (or a combination of them) might have of the activities that will follow. This process is a classic *peeling the onion* or risk analysis activity. For each of the factors affecting the objective the question: So what? is asked and repeated several times for each deduction that is made from each factor. This very repetitive activity is designed to draw everything possible out of the factors. Once the planning team is satisfied that they have drawn everything they can from the consideration of the factors they are able to decide what options are open to them.

Options Open

This element of the assessment process is one of determining the options that are available to the senior leader to respond to a crisis.

In the example of an emerging bushfire crisis the development of Options Open might flow something like this:

> ### The objective is to save human lives.
>
> The number and usability of evacuation routes is a factor.
>
> If there are suitable safe evacuation routes available, then an option to achieve the objective is to evacuate the people who are in threatened areas.

Alternatively, if there are no safe and suitable evacuation routes for the affected people a logical deduction is that evacuating people from the path of the fire front is not an option. In this situation evacuation is not an option that is open and should therefore be eliminated.

Given that the preferred option of evacuation is not available the course of action might be to 'stay and defend'. As this option is now required how can the people be reinforced to give them the best possible chance of survival? Do 'safe havens' exist in the area? Etc., etc.

This process should be continued until a viable option(s) is/are developed (remember whatever the answer it will not be perfect because we would prefer to evacuate the people in the first place).

In the second example used, the consideration of Options may look like the following:

The objective is to avoid a budgetary crisis by introducing new policies to alter current service delivery programs.

The cost of alternative government service delivery options for these programs are prohibitive.

Other non-government service providers are available to deliver the programs at lower costs.

The political risk if the programs are outsourced may be high but not critical.

In this case using alternative government provided programs is not an option that would meet the objective as costs would be even higher. Outsourcing is an option that can be pursued but the political risk must be managed.

By considering all the deductions that have been made through the examination of the factors that affect the objective, several viable options may be determined. A benefit of this process at this stage is that the planning team and the senior leader are now very aware of the context of the situation they confront, the objective of their efforts, the factors that affect the achievement of that objective and what these things collectively mean if the context is changed. Each of the viable options can then be subjected to a further risk analysis if considered necessary.

The process not only logically leads to selecting a preferred option but it also provides essential education for the senior leader. This deep understanding of the characteristics of the crisis that is emerging generates a high level of flexibility as plans can be altered later to meet unexpected problems with a solid knowledge base.

Best Option

The penultimate step in the assessment process is to examine the viable options open and make a choice of the best option that will be used as the basis for all future planning until the process is repeated, perhaps with a modified objective and limitations. The choice of best option is the responsibility of the senior leader, albeit with advice from the planning team that has worked on the crisis response. The senior leader should never delegate this responsibility.

Outline Plan

With all the information that has been derived through the assessment process it is now a relatively simple matter to develop an outline plan. The intent in this step is to give the planning team(s) sufficient guidance to allow them to continue to develop detailed plans once they have received the selected course of action. This method releases the senior leader from the detailed planning process at an appropriate time.

The critical element of the outline plan is, once again, the objective. As the assessment process is applied it is possible that the original objective might have to be reviewed and qualified or altered. Similarly, during the process it might become evident that to achieve the objective, one or two preliminary steps need to be put in place in order to achieve it and therefore several sequential plans may need to be developed.

A tragic but very clear example of what can happen if the objective is not carefully decided upon can be found in the results of a hastily conceived and planned Australian scheme to provide free home insulation (the Home Insulation Program (HIP)).

In the now infamous 'Pink Batts' crisis in Australia during the Global Financial Crisis (GFC) in 2008, a free household insulation program was introduced as one of a series of measures to stimulate parts of the Australian economy. The aim was to use government spending to help prevent Australia from slipping into economic recession. Sadly, the objective of the HIP was only focused on stimulating a part of the economy that had environmental benefits and little attention was paid to other elements. Insufficient attention was paid to ensuring that the program was carried out safely. Installation contractors' lives were lost because of this omission.

> Using the wisdom of hindsight, it is suggested that perhaps the program objective for the HIP might have been:
>
> 'To stimulate the Australian economy by introducing a program of free household roof insulation. The program is to be conducted by qualified installers in a safe manner in accordance with industry standards.'

Adding the limitation relating to safety has the effect of changing the entire rollout of the new government program. It is obvious that this revised program objective would lead to a very different implementation process than using an objective which simply focused on providing free household insulation to homeowners who wanted to take advantage of the new scheme. The use of a thorough assessment process may have assisted in avoiding the tragic outcomes that have now conclusively been linked to the poor planning that was carried out prior to introducing the new home insulation scheme.

Outline Plan Format

Organisations should develop a format for their outline plans so that omissions do not occur. The following simple plan sequence provides a commonly used format.

Outline Plan

Context

Summarise the knowledge leading to the framing of the event and the building of the context of the crisis/problem that has been developed by the senior leader and the crisis response planning team

Objective

Specify the exact objective that the senior leader has selected for the plan to achieve and list any limitations

Conduct

Include the detail of how the Objective is going to be achieved. Tasks should be allocated to organisational elements and the make up of combined teams specified. Leaders should be appointed for all organisational elements formed.

Administrative Matters

Provide details about how the implementation of the plan will be supported to achieve the objective. Include logistic matters (including staffing & budget requirements) and responsibilities allocated.

Coordination

Explain how different elements of the crisis response will be coordinated and how operational communications will be used. Cover media management and public communication systems to be employed during implementation of the plan.

The acronym COCAC can be used as a memory jogger. This acronym has frequently been used in aid and development projects whether they have been an emergency response to a massive disaster (e.g. tsunami or earthquake) or more general aid projects that need detailed plans to ensure successful implementation. It should be remembered that in an emerging crisis, staff can easily become overwhelmed by the workload. Simple memory aids such as a widely understood acronym can assist in these situations.

Examination of the crises in the work leading to this book showed the existence of many plans designed to achieve an overall objective but the plans were often inflexibly applied. A plan that is developed to meet a certain objective and then fails to adapt to variations in planning assumptions or changes to other factors is not likely to succeed. Rather, such a plan is static, a one-time only response that is bound to fail given any variations in elements of the emerging crisis.

Senior leaders must specify planning objectives and limitations very clearly

Chapter 4
Testing Crisis Response Plans

The completion of the crisis response planning process outlined in the previous chapter is only one step in the development of a good plan. Now it needs to be tested to see if it will actually work. The amount of time available to test the plan will dictate the method to be used.

Testing the plan can also allow new senior leaders to educate themselves properly on the process that has led to the development of previous and accepted pre-planned response actions. Newly appointed senior leaders regularly adopt ownership of crisis response plans that have been developed by their predecessors. At high (national or corporate) levels, it is impractical to start the assessment and planning process again every time a senior leader responsible for implementation of a crisis response plan changes. The new senior leader, however, needs to know as much about the plan as the originator of the plan. Testing the plan is the best method of quickly educating the new senior leader. Simply leafing through a written crisis response plan does not build sufficient knowledge for its implementation.

Sadly, another driver of the need for actually testing a crisis response plan is the reality that many plans are developed by staff teams and then passed to the senior leader for approval. The plan is then approved, registered and promulgated as the new source of responsibilities and actions that are to be taken in the event of the plan being activated.

The senior leader has often not participated fully in the planning process (despite this being described as essential in the previous chapter).

Having staff present the previously used assumptions and options for the senior leader's endorsement is a good place for the senior leader to start their direct education in the planning process and testing of the plans. Two other very useful methods are 'red teaming' and 'worst-case scenario planning.'

Red Teaming

Red teaming is a method of testing a scenario or plan. As its name implies, it is an activity conducted by a team formed specifically to stress test the work of a planning team to find errors or weaknesses in assumptions or possible points of failure in a plan.

Members of a red team should *not* have been a part of the planning team which developed the scenario or plan that is to be stress tested. They should be credible staff members who are prepared to take a completely fresh look at the work they are testing. It is recommended that the red team include at least one person from outside the main work area of the organisation which is producing the scenario or plan. For example, if a new government policy is being developed, a community member might be included in the red team. It is important to note that this is not a focus group activity. The task is to stress test work that has already been undertaken by subject matter experts.

Red teams should have a leader appointed who is responsible for developing a methodology for their assessment and for keeping the group's activities directed. Results need to be recorded.

During the red team's consideration, members should be directed to look for errors in thinking, unjustified or erroneous assumptions or planned actions that could easily fail. Additionally, the team should look for any possible unintended consequences that implementation of a plan or policy might cause.

The red team should also test assumptions and plans against what could become an out-of-scale event. This is a good method of identifying and, hopefully reducing, any unconscious bias that has crept into the scenario development or planning process.

Worst-Case Scenario Planning

Every incident that occurs does not require expenditure of the resources necessary to undertake worst-case scenario planning. Routine events can generally be managed by a standard response. This means that pre-planned, rehearsed responses using organic assets will be adequate to contain and remedy the situation.

Fluctuations in the share price of a publicly listed corporation, the response to a minor motor vehicle accident or a problem with an element of public policy should not automatically trigger a response that includes worst-case scenario planning at senior levels of leadership. It is true that junior leaders/managers at levels designed to respond to such issues should be ready to escalate a situation but typically, any escalation occurs after the initial response has been undertaken.

The question that must be asked when an incident occurs is not: How big is this incident? but: What are the possible flow on effects of this incident?

A traffic accident that occurs at a choke point on a major arterial road at peak hour may not involve any injuries to passengers but could lead to traffic chaos that causes unpredictable results, including many other traffic accidents that do cause injuries. Should such an accident occur at a time when there is a highly energised political debate being conducted around traffic management, then the ramifications stemming from this relatively routine response could be disproportionate. In these examples, it may be wise to initiate worst-case scenario planning immediately the potential for flow on effects is observed.

Consider the case of a small bushfire being ignited in dense bush land by a dry lightning strike. While the initial business-as-usual response is being initiated the potential flow on effects of the fire spreading need to be considered. Many factors will impact on the possible need to commence worst-case scenario planning. For example, senior leaders might need to consider factors such as:

- predicted weather conditions
- the level of fuel around the dry lightning strike
- the likely or historic direction of run of the fire should it not be extinguished
- population and infrastructure in the path of the fire and possible changes in direction of run
- environmentally sensitive locations near the location of the fire.

If there are early, unintended consequences when a new government policy is being rolled out it may also be necessary to move to a crisis planning footing to ameliorate and then halt the possible flow on effects of these consequences. The problems that arise in one area may not occur in any other area across the nation but, on the other hand, they might. Are there special situations that have not been factored into the development of the policy? The possible flow on effects of the unintended consequences should be considered and worst-case scenario planning may need to be undertaken.

Deepwater Horizon Disaster, Gulf of Mexico, 2010.

Conducting Worst-Case Scenario Planning

Worst-case scenario planning is typically undertaken simultaneously with a pre-planned response to a crisis. Senior leaders delegate leadership of the initial incident response to others (while retaining oversight) and initiate consideration of the actions that may be required as a result of an unanticipated escalation of the size of the incident. Worst-case scenario planning should, as a guide, be undertaken when dealing with major incidents. It may even be advisable to have a special team ready to undertake this extra planning work while other planners are busy responding to the emerging needs of the response.

For this book incidents can be categorised into routine, major or catastrophic. Other categorisations may be used but these three serve the purpose to develop the concept of worst-case scenario planning. When a major incident occurs, it is suggested that senior leaders should initiate worst-case scenario planning.

A preliminary activity to worst-case scenario planning is, therefore, to develop a method of categorising types of incidents into what are considered routine, major or catastrophic events. This categorisation should be developed and published within organisations after consultation. It may then be shared with other related organisations if this is appropriate. This work helps markedly in establishing a common language and understanding of the basis of incident management and responsibilities in an organisation.

Many readers may now be saying that this work of categorisation is, in fact, a simplification process and therefore unconscious bias (see Chapter 1—Framing the Event) is going to be an introduced risk into this process. Routine incidents can, of course, quickly become major incidents and if senior leaders are not paying attention then very poor responses to an escalating situation can easily occur. The important point is that a system must be in place to identify and communicate any transition from one incident level to another to the organisation's senior leadership.

A typical worst-case scenario planning activity begins with the outline plan developed for the response to the possible or emerging crisis. From this starting point, the context can be varied upwards to show an escalation to a point well above the level of the currently expected maximum response required.

Assumptions can be varied and the outline plan tested. The planning team examines the plan to see if it can accommodate an escalating situation and up to what point this escalation can be met by the proposed plan. Once the point is reached that the current plan cannot be considered effective as a response plan then the timing for the production of an updated plan can be determined and promulgated. If the current plan cannot cater for a degree of escalation then it will need to be rewritten immediately.

Senior leaders again need to participate directly in this planning process. It is imperative that this personal involvement takes place because, as already stated, planning is a process of education. A worst-case scenario will inevitably involve many other people and possibly many other organisations. It is not sufficient for senior leaders to delegate this level of planning to subordinates and to then simply pass the plans on as being theirs—no matter how good their subordinates are. Involve the subordinate planners in the work by all means, but senior leaders must participate themselves.

In worst-case scenario planning the factors that are impacting on a given major incident are not determined by the current, known situation. Rather, they are derived from a series of 'what if' questions. Questions are asked such as: What if torrential rain continued to fall for several days? or: What if the fire broke containment lines unexpectedly and extreme winds picked up?

These 'what if' questions need to be wide ranging and need to challenge conventional thinking and existing forecasts—be they environmental, financial, economic or social. Personal participation by senior leaders in this element of the planning process ensures that they understand the assumptions that are being made and that they are well informed about the possible implications of these factors impacting on the incident to which they are planning a response.

Crisis Response Plan Training

This process can also be used in training scenarios to build knowledge and expertise within the senior leadership team of any organisation.

Taking time out from day to day leadership activities to participate in hypothetical planning scenarios, with staff responsible for detailed planning activities, is an excellent way to prepare for a future crisis.

As each of the 'what if' questions are asked and the appropriate response plans outlined, it becomes possible to build a series of contingency plans. These can be used to initiate the escalation of a response should a major incident be impacted by additional factors that increase the potential of it becoming a catastrophic event. Senior leaders in the organisation will understand what resources and actions will be required to respond to an escalating crisis. Resources can be identified in advance and assets warned that they may be called upon to assist in a response.

After a plan or scenario has been red teamed and possibly subjected to a worst-case scenario test, the senior leader can have confidence that it is ready to be tested during an exercise. This could be a desk top exercise or a full, scenario-driven activity that requires everyone involved to stop routine activities and implement the plan as if they were responding to a real crisis.

Normal business will still need to be managed during the conduct of an exercise. The senior leader may therefore opt to put various elements of their organisation through the implementation of the sections of the plan for which they are responsible separately.

After the plan or scenario has been exercised it is essential that any lessons are identified, analysed and if necessary, used to modify the plan. Only by completing this process can the senior leader can be assured that the lessons have, indeed, been learnt.

PART 2
ORGANISATIONAL
LEADERSHIP TECHNIQUES

A leader...is like a shepherd. He stays behind the flock, letting the most nimble go out ahead, whereupon the others follow, not realizing that all along they are being directed from behind.

Nelson Mandela

CHAPTER 5
DISTRIBUTED LEADERSHIP

During a crisis the senior leader(s) will be stretched to the limit. It is essential that everyone in the organisation does their very best to overcome the enormous challenges that must be faced and responded to. It is impossible for a senior leader alone to carry the burden of all the decisions that are necessary in a crisis.

A simple methodology can be employed by senior leaders in large organisations to manage an escalating crisis when an immediate team response is required. It is known as 'distributed leadership'.

This senior leadership tool has been used in military organisations for many years. It is possible that the tool originated there but its use has been evident in other successful public sector and large private sector organisations over a very long period. Military organisations have modified the process many times and rebadged it constantly. Notwithstanding these cosmetic changes, the basic process remains untouched and is elegant in its simplicity (the military generally refer to this process as directive control).

Engaging Teams During a Crisis

The distributed leadership process may be applied to senior leadership situations in any large organisation. It requires the senior leader to follow five steps:

1. Clearly state the objective(s) to be achieved and allocate these to individuals
2. Allocate resources to organisational elements to achieve the senior leader's objective(s)
3. Provide subordinates with boundaries for their responsibilities
4. Allow subordinates to plan their own actions to achieve their objective(s) with the resources allocated
5. Establish reporting requirements to ensure that the senior leader maintains situational awareness.

The process brings teams together, displays trust and shows respect for the experience and talent that already exists in an organisation. The senior leader is better able to manage the multiple demands on their limited time during a crisis and is also better able to harness the total thinking power and effort of their organisation to combat the crisis or change they are confronting.

The distributed leadership process may be a common-sense approach but it is not easy to implement if the senior leader has not practised it. For this process to work effectively, the senior leader must take a risk and trust their subordinates to get on with the work of planning their own actions within the limitations imposed upon them. Some senior leaders find this a difficult thing to do. If the senior leader is prone to micro-management, the notion of allowing subordinates to plan their own actions in response to a crisis will probably be an anathema.

Developing the required level of trust in subordinate teams for the implementation of the distributed leadership process is something that should be a mandatory requirement for all senior leaders. Those not naturally predisposed to giving subordinates their trust will need to set and run training to allow themselves to build that level of trust. If subordinates cannot be trusted to plan their own actions after this training, then either the training has not met its aim or the subordinate teams are unsuitable for the responsibilities that they have. Either way, the senior leader has a decision to make.

Managing Senior Leadership Transitions

When senior leaders move into their jobs they have usually given thought to just how they will go about achieving the many tasks before them. They will have thought about their priorities (many of these will have been given to them by their superiors) and what they want their teams to achieve. Unless this thinking is around a brand new senior position in a brand-new organisation there will also be legacy issues to deal with. The new leader might have to step into a predecessor's very 'big shoes' and there may be strong residual loyalty to the predecessor that will need to be redirected to the new senior leader.

From the subordinates' perspective there will be an element of apprehension. How will the new boss operate? Will they be a micro-manager? Will they want to reorganise everything? Will the new boss steer the organisation in an entirely unfamiliar direction? These uncertainties all contribute to a reduction in the productivity of the organisation.

Should a crisis confront the organisation close to a senior leadership change, a real risk of sub-optimal performance will exist. This will affect the way in which the organisation responds to the crisis and its plans for the subsequent recovery efforts. If a senior leadership change occurs immediately post a crisis, then parts of the organisation might resist or reject the newcomer unless they have active roles in shaping the organisation to be more effective and resilient in any future crisis.

A new senior leader can gain immediate respect if they introduce distributed leadership when they assume their new role. Spreading responsibility for decision making throughout their organisation ameliorates many of the apprehensions that develop in organisations at the time of a senior leadership transition.

Implementing Distributed Leadership

Clearly State the Objective(s)

This is a critical first step in the distributed leadership process. If the senior leader gets this wrong the whole organisation could end up focusing on the wrong issues. Selecting the objective(s) for the distributed leadership process is not as simple as the senior leader making an 'educated guess'. The objective(s) should be derived from the deductive assessment activity that is a part of the planning process (see Chapter 3—Crisis Response Planning Process).

Like all objectives in any organisation, they should be both achievable and measurable. The senior leader must give careful thought to whether an objective can, in fact, be achieved given the situation faced, any limitations that have been imposed (e.g. time), the resources available and skills and capacity of the people in the response area. The objective(s) must be unambiguous. There is no room in a crisis response for misunderstanding. There will be more than enough uncertainty facing an organisation as a crisis unfolds and internal misunderstandings must be avoided at all costs.

Emergency Services need clear objectives for an effective response.

Allocate Resources

The saying 'there are never enough resources' will always apply in a crisis. Therefore, one of the key tasks for a senior leader is the identification and distribution of resources to parts of their organisation so they can confront the challenges they face. The senior leader should anticipate some resource bidding to occur from various parts of their organisation. Some subordinates will be better negotiators than others and the senior leader needs to understand who are the most persuasive members of their organisation. The senior leader must, however, control any resource bidding that might occur and quickly reach a final determination. Subordinates can then be directed to develop their individual plans of action.

A good senior leadership tool is the use of a regular *resource allocation review*. In these reviews the senior leader can reallocate resources according to the reporting that subordinates make regarding their achievement of the objective(s) they have been given. Subordinates, knowing that these regular reviews will occur, are then able to gather the data and arguments that they think might persuade the senior leader to vary initial resource allocations and present them at future reviews.

It is important that the senior leader properly understands just what capabilities are at the disposal of their organisation. This applies to capabilities that are both inside and outside the organisation. There may be alternative sources of capability available from other organisations or from within the organisation itself. Understanding an organisation's capabilities and those in other organisations that may also be involved in the same emerging crisis, is an important part of any senior leader's role. This is discussed more fully in Chapter 8—Identifying Organisational Capabilities.

It is too late to begin identifying missing or hidden capability resources when a crisis is unfolding. The senior leader must work on capability identification and assessment from their very first day in the job. They also need to collaborate with external organisations to understand exactly what their capabilities are and so determine whether they might provide additional resources to assist in the response to a crisis.

Provide Boundaries

Subordinates must be told what the limits of their responsibilities are if they are to respond effectively to a crisis. Each subordinate also needs to know what boundaries have been given to colleagues. In this way subordinates can focus their efforts and build plans to meet the objective(s) they have been given. They will work in unison with other colleagues and they will not find that they are conflicting with other plans and activities.

Boundaries can take many forms. For example, the boundaries used in the distributed leadership process might be geographical, financial, temporal or environmental.

Allow subordinates to plan their own actions

Once the objective(s) and resource allocations are made and boundaries are established, the senior leader should step back and allow subordinates to make their own plans to respond to the elements of the crisis they have been directed to deal with. Each subordinate will go about this process differently but the overall outcomes in terms of the planning process should be fully in accordance with the senior leader's objective(s). Some subordinate leaders will also need to use the distributed leadership process to direct the actions of elements of their own teams. The planning process that is outlined in Chapter 3 should also guide the subordinate processes.

The outcome of this distributed leadership effort is the maximisation of the potential of the whole organisation. Subordinates will also feel that they are truly being valued and they will be highly motivated to do the very best job that they can.

Establish reporting requirements

A senior leader cannot be left wondering what is happening after subordinates begin to implement their respective plans. Regular but simple reporting systems need to be used to ensure that the senior leader can maintain situational awareness (see Chapter 2—Thinking Strategically). In Chapter 3—Crisis Response Planning it is stressed that plans must be flexible to be able to respond to changes in the situation that is being faced. Objectives must be modified, resources redirected, and boundaries may be altered as the crisis response continues. Changes to objectives are the senior leader's responsibility and therefore they must be kept informed through accurate and timely reporting.

When employing the distributed leadership process the senior leader must test the level of understanding that exists between themselves and their subordinates. The senior leader might think that they excel in clarity of expression but the stresses of an emerging crisis, unconscious bias and other factors all conspire to create misunderstanding. The senior leader should require subordinates to brief them verbally on their understanding ('back briefing' is a common term for this activity) of the instructions that they have been given.

Distributed leadership is a very effective technique. It is equally applicable to days of routine activity and times of crisis. Properly implemented, it will give the senior leader the capacity to build their situational awareness and to manage the 'big picture'. This process also helps remove the temptation for the senior leader to engage at the technical level and thereby run the real risk of micro-managing and failing to frame an event accurately. Typically, senior leaders have been promoted through the various levels of their industry and have been highly successful at each of these levels. Their comfort zone is in these technical areas. This is especially so with the newly appointed senior leader. Employing distributed leadership provides a means to move into a new comfort zone.

Chapter 6
Establishing Role Clarity

Ensuring that everyone in the organisation knows exactly what he or she is responsible and accountable for seems to be a self-evident requirement of organisational design. Similarly, there is an obvious need for staff in any organisation to know what roles their colleagues are responsible for fulfilling. Role clarity is an essential prerequisite for an effective crisis response.

Typically, organisations will produce some form of duty statement or role description that is intended to outline, in a succinct form, what roles various staff members are required to carry out. On occasions these documents are prepared to assist in the recruitment of staff.

The preparation of such documents is a major project for a large organisation and is usually undertaken by specialist human resources (HR) staff. HR specialists understand issues of determining the work value of positions, appropriate pre-requisite qualifications needed by the staff, lines of reporting and many other matters concerning the role. When they are produced, these role descriptions are an accurate reflection of how employees will work in an organisation. However, these documents become outdated quite quickly.

Some HR specialists become so involved in the writing of duty statements that their development becomes a full-time job and the product becomes an unwieldly document that is impossible to maintain. This is of little use to a senior leader. The use of role descriptions has been a very successful modification to the traditional duty statement approach.

There are five elements that should be present in a useful role description that will allow a senior leader to ensure that role clarity exists within their organisation. The five elements that are suggested are:

- Purpose of position
- Dimensions and context of position
- Key accountabilities
- Performance indicators
- Experience, skills and qualifications required

All five of these elements should be able to be contained on a single page. There should be no more than five to seven key accountabilities and three to five performance indicators.

A preliminary step for the HR staff is the identification of the work streams or job families that are required in the organisation. The senior leader should direct that work stream/job family mapping be completed as an essential prerequisite to establishing role descriptions and hence role clarity in their organisation. The HR staff can then assist the senior leader by drafting role descriptions.

The senior leader must exercise strong direction over the HR staff in the organisation at this stage. The outcomes of this work have direct operational implications and must not be left to HR staff members to complete when time allows between managing promotions, leave approvals, redresses, and so on.

When the role descriptions have been completed a final check should be made of actual activity against the now established role. The individuals occupying the various roles examined need to be fully engaged in this process and they need to also have a degree of ownership of their role description.

Organisations should be living, organic entities and therefore it should be expected that roles will change. Such changes need to be approved and documented in the promulgated role descriptions as part of an ongoing process.

Example Role Description Document

Employment Stream: Off-Shore Safety Management **Position: Specialist Off-Shore Safety Director–Level 3** **Reports: All Level 2 and Level 1 Off-Shore Safety Managers**

Purpose:	
Technical expert recognised throughout the organisation. Raises level of understanding of their technical area and the implications for safety systems in the off-shore exploration environment	
Key Accountabilities:	**Performance Indicators:**
• Leads regulatory oversight activities • Provides technical/safety systems leadership to the organisation • Maintains insight into global safety system trends • Mentors staff on the implementation of safety systems • Drafts safety policies related to off-shore exploration activities	• Safety requirements adhered to at all times by off-shore crews • Organisation recognised by peers as a leader in safety in off-shore operations • Regulatory requirements met or exceeded by all operational sites
Dimensions and Context:	**Experience, Skills and Qualifications:**
• Safety systems leadership in constantly evolving technical domains • Complexity of relationship between the organisation, its multiple stakeholders and regulators	• Postgraduate degree in field • Minimum of 10-15 years industry and regulatory experience • Significant experience in off-shore safety areas

Once the Level 3 (there may be higher levels in some fields) role is described, then role descriptions for the subordinate Level 2 and Level 1 positions should be drafted using a similar format. Each work stream should have role descriptions developed.

Performance Management

A crisis response requires everyone in an organisation to perform at their best. Performance management is, therefore, a key senior leadership responsibility.

Flattened banana plantation in north Queensland after Cyclone Yasi struck.

Performance management, particularly of poor performance, is not always well done. Often the reason for this is inadequate clarity around just what is expected of incumbents in various positions. The use of the role description outlined above will assist in providing a good basis for performance management before a crisis emerges.

Long and detailed duty statements are a recipe for debate and unpleasantness when performance reviews are conducted. As already mentioned, organisations are constantly evolving and therefore a long and detailed list of duties will quickly become outdated creating a potentially difficult performance management situation. Individuals are more easily able to review a succinct role description on a regular basis and pass suggested revisions to HR staff for consideration. Significant changes should be referred to the relevant senior leader for approval.

Regular performance management meetings should be a chance for staff to interact directly with their senior leaders. However, regular performance interactions are often rare events. Instead, the performance management meeting only occurs when something has gone wrong and the senior leader intervenes as a rectification step.

It is little wonder then that performance management meetings are frequently viewed as disciplinary actions as opposed to a chance to have a discussion with the senior leader about the job and genuinely reflect on how the incumbent is 'travelling'. The senior leader should additionally be searching for any barriers to the individual's performance that they could remove. Carried out properly, the performance management meeting can become a really positive interaction—even if the incumbent whose performance is being examined leaves the meeting with several 'areas required for improvement'.

For a successful performance management system to operate it is essential that these face to face meetings actually occur. Nothing damages the system more than the senior leader cancelling performance management meetings regularly because they claim they are too busy. The senior leader is going to rely on these same staff to assist in resolving a crisis response should that be required. Preparing staff to be at their best in a crisis is what a senior leader must do constantly. A senior leader must therefore assign a very high priority to performance management meetings with their staff.

Intelligence:

...the result of the process of acquiring, storing in memory, retrieving, combining, comparing, and using in new contexts information and cognitive skills[1]

Humphreys, L. G.
The Construction of General/Intelligence.

CHAPTER 7
DEVELOPING INTELLIGENCE

The product of the process where skilled analysts take information and convert it into usable material is intelligence. It is critical that leaders understand this and do not fall into the trap of taking a single, unanalysed piece of information as intelligence to use as the basis for decision-making.

Today, leaders in all fields are literally bombarded with information from many sources. The obvious challenge is to decide which sources of information should be fed into the process of creating intelligence. The Web has created both a wonderful source of information for processing, and simultaneously, a source of misinformation that confounds the intelligence process. The term 'fake news' has been introduced into our leadership lexicon. 'Misinformation' is another term we are now familiar with.

How does a leader deal with this torrent of inputs and separate the real information from the false information?

Firstly, leaders today need to develop *trusted sources* of information. These trusted sources are ones that the leader is confident will provide information that is as accurate as possible by checking sources, using multiple models to develop predictions or always corroborate information before disseminating it.

Secondly, in the process of developing knowledge of trusted sources, the senior leader should also make themselves aware of the reverse—

those sources that they do not trust. There are now many sources of deliberate misinformation that can find their way into the intelligence process. Intelligence staff and information management teams now always need to be alert to the need to identify sites pushing misinformation to satisfy a particular agenda.

As these sources of misinformation are identified, all staff in the organisation should be made aware that they should not use information from them in their planning and crisis response operations. These sites must, however, be monitored as they will become sources of information to communities that do not recognise them as pushing misinformation. When such sites are identified the intelligence/information management team must be advised so that they can take steps to counter the misinformation that is circulating.

The transfer of intelligence from one group/agency to another must also be assessed and not taken for granted. Unless the leader is satisfied that the intelligence being passed on is the result of analysing trustworthy information it should be rejected, at least until it has been corroborated.

Senior leaders must establish a set of simple criteria that both they and their teams can use to establish the veracity of the intelligence/information they feed into the larger Intelligence process.

Trusted Sources

There is no such thing as an infallible source. Everyone can, and will, at times make mistakes. The question here, though, is: 'Who can we trust to make strenuous efforts, using respected processes, to produce information that we can rely on the be correct in most cases?' We need to understand the elements of the information that may be subject to variation. We also need to be aware of alternative modelling that can be undertaken and the implications of alternative models.

Generally, leaders can rely on government reports/analyses that look at historical data sets. The use of this data can be examined and compared, the process of analysis can be understood and questioned if need be. In Australia, it is reasonable to assign a relatively high level of trust to analyses by agencies such as the Treasury, the Australian Bureau of Statistics (ABS) and the Bureau of Meteorology (BoM). This is not to say that mistakes have not been made by such agencies but rather that a high level of analytical skill exists in them and the analysis of historical data sets is generally not impacted on by the political process.

Information analysts or intelligence officers need to understand any weaknesses that trusted sources may have in their modelling and prediction techniques. The managers of the Wivenhoe Dam excess water release that caused extensive flooding in Brisbane have publicly stated that they did not have high levels of trust in BoM weather forecasts. This led them to discount predictions of extremely heavy rain in their catchment area. Consequently, they did not manage preventative controlled releases of water in the dam to create capacity for the predicted rainfall and avoid 'over topping' the reservoir.

The impact of the political process on data sets needs further elaboration. This term is not meant to imply a deliberate distortion of data but rather to say that there are times when, for example, data might have been produced using different methods from those used for many years and that this different analysis comes about because of a political direction. The reason for the political direction is irrelevant. What is important is that the year-on-year trend analysis is broken and previously reliable sources of information become unreliable as they may only represent one year of data analysis under the 'new' method.

The so-called 'central agencies' of government routinely produce estimates. When called upon to produce estimates for the future, the analysts in these agencies usually produce a range of outcomes and present these to the government of the day. The government, not the analysts, selects that point in the range of estimates presented that they will use to produce their forward-looking policies. History has shown that frequently the estimates used to support the adoption of new government policies are at the optimistic end of the range. Such estimates should be used by senior leaders with great care when producing their intelligence.

Criteria for Assessing Information

Information should be assessed by asking questions such as:

- Is this a primary source of information or is it hearsay, assumption or from a secondary/tertiary source?
- Can this information be corroborated by another source?
- What is the actual date and time that this information was produced?
- What deductions are likely to be made if this information is used and therefore how important is it in the intelligence process?
- Are there parties who will receive direct benefit from its use in the intelligence process?

Information must not simply be accepted at face value. By developing a series of minimum questions that need to be applied to all information flowing into a crisis management team, the team can have a higher level of confidence that they are acting on sound data and not noise generated by various sources as a crisis emerges. Through processes like this information is converted into intelligence.

Local Knowledge in Intelligence

When considering many of the disasters that have occurred over the past decade or so, it is apparent that there has been a real dilution of the importance of local knowledge. The centralisation of control in almost all out-of-scale events has made it more difficult for local knowledge to reach the ears of senior leaders in charge of the response to these events.

> In the Canberra bushfires of January 2003, a local ACT Rural Fire Service brigade captain at Tharwa, a small, village in the south of the Territory, became very concerned about the threat that the raging fires posed. Years of experience told him that the nature of the fire front's progress would inevitably lead to the destruction of large parts of the village if not the complete razing of the settlement and the rural properties surrounding it.

The brigade captain requested approval from his headquarters to begin the controlled burning of a firebreak to protect the village. This request was repeatedly refused. Equipped with years of experience and therefore local knowledge the brigade captain ignored the refusal of his request by his headquarters and initiated the controlled burn. The village was saved.

Aerial firefighting helicopter, Canberra.

This situation illustrates the problem that senior leaders can have with collecting, collating and disseminating intelligence that comes to them. The central headquarters was itself being threatened by the fires. The conventional wisdom was to concentrate resources in other areas based on the intelligence that was flowing in. Political leaders and emergency managers were stunned by the ferocity of the fires that had impacted the suburbs on the north western urban edge of the National Capital and were not focused as much on the southern area of Tharwa. Further, local knowledge was not held in the high regard that it should have been.

Here was a chance to save lives and property but the focus was on the results of damage that had already been done. The actions of a very experienced brigade captain were effective and subsequent after-action reviews vindicated him. More importantly, this allowed the lesson to be incorporated into legislation dealing with emergency responses in the ACT. Intelligence gleaned from local knowledge was elevated to the highest importance in this legislation.

Knowing What is Changing from Normal

The onset of a crisis is not the time to be trying to determine what normal looks like. Members of staff employed to build an intelligence picture need to be working in this area full time. They need to be developing a clear understanding of what normal looks like so that they can detect shifts from the normal state. This type of activity is common in the industrial/ technological world as agile companies need to be able to respond rapidly to a competitor's sudden innovation or change in business direction. The same agility is required in government agencies and emergency management organisations.

All agencies are exposed to a high level of risk if they cannot clearly articulate the components of the normal state in their area of work. For example, energy supply is a major factor driving investment in many sectors. The issue of renewables has introduced a new dynamic into this equation and this is all in an environment of emissions management and very rapid changes in energy storage systems such as lithium batteries and pumped hydro power. Add to this complex area the fact that most power generation and distribution in developed countries is now run by private enterprise with a profit motive, it is difficult for government agencies to describe the current normal state of the energy production and distribution system in their geographic area.

All of this means that governments must employ people who are skilled in assessing all of the factors that combine to produce the normal state of the energy system. People who are capable of developing policies to move forward into the future must also be employed. Without these people, a crisis is sure to occur. Sadly, there is not a lot of evidence in the developed world that governments have taken this risk seriously. An energy policy crisis now exists in many countries and the economic cost of this is likely to be huge.

Water supply is another resource area that requires skilled analysis by trained intelligence staff to develop and maintain a view of what is the normal state. Current holding capacity is somewhat easier to measure than some aspects of an energy system but, obviously, the water supply system is dependent to a large degree on weather. While desalination plants exist in many coastal areas, huge storage and distribution issues exist in arid inland areas. In Australia, some very large irrigation projects consume vast amounts of water that is desperately needed to be shared downstream.

A very large and public project to develop a water plan for the Murray-Darling Basin in Australia appeared to produce a starting point for assessing a 'new normal'. Very recently, however, media reporting has exposed serious flaws in the implementation of this plan and reporting has even pointed to government complicity in some actions that have been taken to avoid full compliance with the plan.

The build-up of forest fire fuel is another area that staff in the emergency services need to be knowledgeable about what is normal and what is not. The normal state is critical intelligence against which changes can be measured and the appropriate steps taken to prepare a response before a crisis occurs in the form of a catastrophic bushfire.

In the financial sector markets fluctuate constantly. There is a normality to these fluctuations and this sector is now generally well prepared to manage crises in a relatively volatile environment by applying appropriate algorithms and by engaging experienced analysts. Of course, this should be the case after the experience of the Global Financial Crisis (GFC) of 2008.

In every sector, it is important to establish just what is normal and what is starting to push outside of the current normal. This task needs to be undertaken by trained intelligence staff and they should have the respect and access required to ensure that when they begin to see abnormal signs in their field of expertise, they can quickly brief senior leaders who take their assessments seriously.

It is also essential that organisations that are focussing on an emerging problem maintain an awareness of developments in inter-related areas. The management of water catchments in areas which have experienced abnormally low rainfall or even drought are a good example of how the overwhelming desire to fill dams and rivers can lead to senior managers not identifying information that might cause them to alter their decision-making process.

> In June 2016 Tasmania's energy company, Hydro Tasmania, conducted a pre-planned cloud seeding operation to increase rainfall over one of its major water catchment areas which is a component of the state's hydroelectricity generating system.
>
> The cloud seeding operation was conducted on a day when the Bureau of Meteorology had issued major flood warnings in the area as a result of approaching severe storms.
>
> The day after the cloud seeding occurred the catchment area experienced severe flooding and a massive emergency response operation was required.
>
> Lives were lost and infrastructure was damaged. Hydro Tasmania's corporate reputation was severely damaged.

There was no apparent framing of the event undertaken by senior leaders in Hydro Tasmania. The situation was not normal and the available information should have alerted the planners of the cloud seeding operations to the high level of risk faced if they proceeded.

Managing Intelligence During a Crisis

Crises usually emerge very quickly even though their origins may be long in the making. As a crisis unfolds there is always an accompanying deluge of information arriving in the senior leader's inbox. Much of this information will be inaccurate and other elements will be highly localised. Little, if any, will be intelligence as the information will not have been analysed, corroborated or assessed by appropriately skilled staff members.

The processing of information into intelligence during a crisis must occur very quickly. This reinforces the need to maintain competent staff during

Water supply crises are increasing in frequency.

normal operating conditions so that they are better positioned to understand what constitutes the 'normal state'. They can then establish collaborative relationships with trusted sources of information/intelligence that can be instantly activated when a crisis occurs. Speed is of the essence and therefore every effort must be made by senior leaders to have an organisational design and operating model that allows activity areas such as intelligence to be easily able to step up from normal to crisis mode without a major reorganisation and the addition of inexperienced staff to this critical area.

Social media will play an increasingly important role in the receipt of information and the subsequent dissemination of intelligence. Intelligence staff must therefore be adept at understanding and managing these forms of communication. Fortunately, the pervasiveness of the various social media platforms means that most staff members in an organisation will be familiar with their use. Staff may not, however, be familiar with the use of social media platforms for the dissemination of misinformation, even though this is becoming more common year by year.

As mentioned previously in this section, misinformation can be fed into the intelligence process very easily. Training needs to be conducted to ensure that intelligence staff can identify misinformation and keep it separate from the information from trusted sources that are being used to produce intelligence about the current crisis.

Once misinformation has been detected and confirmed during a crisis (or during normal state activities) it should be dealt with and not simply discarded. Some of the misinformation will have been generated by the confusion that surrounds any crisis. Other misinformation may be identified as malicious. When this occurs, the senior leader needs to act to have that source closed or, depending on the nature of the misinformation, pass the details to law enforcement officials for action.

Dissemination

In several of the disasters examined, internal clearance processes unnecessarily delayed the release of important information/intelligence to communities and other stakeholders. These process delays meant that communities were put at risk.

Implicit in this is the need for operational areas of organisations to have strong links with a variety of media elements and for those links to be built on a level of trust. In a crisis, all forms of media need to be seen as partners in the response and not as a burden that must be tolerated. If this relationship is established, then the media in all its many forms can become both an essential addition to a senior leader's situational awareness and a tool for clear communication.

Organisational intelligence management units must routinely use processes that are designed for working in a crisis and that can be 'stepped down' to manage routine operations. The size of an intelligence management unit can only be upscaled during a crisis if the processes are already in place for crisis operations and are well practised. Additional staff needed to upscale must be identified and trained in advance if the upscaling is to proceed smoothly.

CHAPTER 8
MANAGING ORGANISATIONAL
RESOURCES

A frequently heard statement in relation to resource management when developing lessons learnt after a crisis is that: "resources were made available but not used in the crisis response." Such statements are coupled with high levels of frustration bordering, at times, on outright anger.

In the 2003 Canberra bushfires off duty firefighters voluntarily reported for duty sensing that they were going to be urgently needed. Initially, they were turned away as managers had not realised the scale of the event that they were facing and, they were worried that there was insufficient budget to pay overtime.

In a bushfire crisis in the Blue Mountains in New South Wales the Australian Defence Force (ADF) had been called out to assist fire fighters with communications and transport support, particularly water tankers as water supply was very difficult in the area around the fires. Several hours after a large ADF convoy of full water tankers arrived at an assembly area close to the fire front they were still parked there 'nose-to-tail' without any call forward or other instructions. At the fire front, tankers were exhausting their on-board water supplies. Just in time, a water-bombing helicopter pilot saw the stationary convoy and arranged for it to start moving forward to replenish empty water tanks. This was a close call but the quick thinking of the helicopter pilot allowed the situation to be brought under control.

Senior leaders must be prepared to deal with resource management issues like those highlighted here. There will be staff members who are specialists in resource management/logistics, however, the presence of these specialists does not allow senior leaders to delegate the responsibility for strategic resource decision-making to them.

What then are the key elements of managing organisational resources on which a leader must concentrate in their preparation to manage a crisis? This important task is more than just ensuring that resources are placed at the right place at the right time. There are eight elements of organisational resource management that, no matter what their backgrounds are, a successful leader must fully understand before being involved in a real crisis. These are:

- organisational capability
- collaboration
- formal and informal organisations
- organisational politics
- staff capability for 24/7 operations
- adequacy of routine maintenance
- interoperability and connectivity
- anticipation

Organisational Capability

Organisations have a reputation and history. A leader entering an existing organisation will have made many assumptions about the organisation before accepting a leadership position in it. If the leader is tasked with creating a new organisation then they will most likely have a clear view of what the new organisation will look like and what it will be able to achieve after establishment and 'bedding in'.

It is essential that these assumptions are tested as soon as possible and either validated or discarded. If validation is not undertaken, then the leader will allow their assumptions about the organisation to become a reality and this may have disastrous consequences.

During a consulting project in the aviation sector I was examining the availability of qualified staff to fill new safety inspector positions that had been created in a major reorganisation. Only two positions were filled and advertisements had been placed to fill the vacant positions. Considerable time had elapsed since the advertisements were released and no suitable applicants had come forward for interview. Further investigation revealed that the educational institutions that had previously produced graduates qualified to fill the new positions had ceased to run the necessary courses. The reorganisation was based on an invalid assumption that the supply of qualified candidates was continuing as before. Major changes had to be made urgently to ensure operational capability was maintained.

It is imperative that leaders undertake formal capability assessments of their organisation at regular intervals (e.g. biennial or triennial assessments). If the leader is new, then it is advisable to conduct a capability assessment as one of the first actions taken on assuming the leadership role.

In its simplest form the capability assessment involves an examination of each of the key functions and elements of an organisation and the drawing of conclusions about their effectiveness. The conclusions can be drawn by conducting on-site interviews and checks, setting activities to be conducted and by comparing elements of the organisation with similar organisational elements in other organisations that have credibility.

The key functions and elements that require their capabilities to be assessed by the senior leader might comprise some, all or more of:

- People
  - key positions filled/unfilled
  - qualifications and skills assessed
  - role descriptions current and understood
  - performance management system in place and active
  - executive commitment and performance management in place

- Policies
  - current policies effective
  - new policies under development meeting timelines
  - policy costing procedures accurate and used
  - adequate consultation being undertaken
  - old policies rescinded when no longer applicable
- ICT
  - systems 'fit for purpose'
  - system updates current
  - system security safeguards (including attempted hacking detection) in place
  - social media management policies appropriate, in place and understood
  - media relationships established
  - compatibility with any organisations likely to provide assistance in a crisis assured
- Equipment
  - all 'fit for purpose'
  - maintenance programs up to date
  - spare parts shortages identified and rectification in progress
  - compatibility with any organisations likely to provide assistance in a crisis assured
  - training programs for operators current and active
  - ability of outsourced contractors to meet surge requirements assured
- Finances
  - all financial guidance and regulations complied with
  - financial reporting processes in place and meeting legal requirements
  - budget allocation sufficient to meet needs of the organisation
  - budget preparation process robust
  - financial delegations and responsibilities understood
- Safety
  - appropriate safety systems in place and understood
  - all relevant legal/duty of care requirements met by safety systems
  - safety awareness established and maintained throughout the organisation
  - safety responsibilities clearly allocated and understood

A senior leader will not be able to do all of these tasks by themselves. There will simply not be enough hours in the day to undertake a capability assessment, conduct planning, complete performance reviews of direct reports, as well as respond to day to day tasks. Add the prospect of responding to a crisis and the senior leader is overloaded.

However, the senior leader does not have to undertake a full capability assessment personally. Many elements can be delegated to others. What is critical is that the senior leader should personally drive the conduct of the capability assessment. This very important task should not be left to others to design and complete. Frequently, consulting organisations are called upon to do this work. That is reasonable provided the strict requirement for the senior leader to designate the capabilities assessed and what specific items are to checked is met.

Senior leaders who allow other executives in their organisation or consultants to use a template to conduct the capability assessment are not meeting their responsibilities. The senior leader must design the plan and the process and then direct others to conduct the detailed work with reports provided to the senior leader as specified.

In some organisations it is possible to run training scenarios to test the ability of the organisation to respond to a crisis. This is a very effective way to measure organisational capability. Training scenarios do require considerable effort to prepare and execute so it may not be possible to exercise the entire organisation at one time. In this case, the various elements of the organisation can be tested separately and then conclusions drawn regarding the whole organisation. This is not as effective as putting the entire organisation through a common scenario that simulates a crisis but it is very worthwhile.

In addition to testing an organisation on a specific scenario(s) it is necessary to assess the capability of the human capital in the organisation. Some assessments can be made during a scenario-driven exercise but a leader must go further. The leader needs to understand the level of qualifications held by staff and the practical experience they have had in the field.

All organisations need a budget to operate. A healthy financial situation is essential to a high level of operational capability. It is a truism that all organisations would like more money to spend on themselves but the question that needs to be asked during a capability assessment is: Do we have enough money to prepare for a crisis and to then see us through the crisis? If the answer is 'yes' to both elements of this question, the organisation is probably on a sound financial footing.

Safety is a critical capability in many organisations tasked with crisis response. This is especially so in emergency management organisations, aviation and other transport industries, mining, the military and the emergency departments of the health system. Such organisations need to constantly review and assess the safety systems they have in place and the ever-changing regulatory environment in which they operate.

After these elements of the organisation have been evaluated, a matrix can be constructed showing the elements and areas that need attention. Actions can then be planned to bring them up to the standard required to run the organisation effectively and to manage the emergence of a crisis.

The final step in conducting a capability assessment is to examine other organisations that might offer assistance during a crisis to understand better just what capabilities they can offer. Obviously, the leader cannot step into another organisation and start conducing their own capability assessment. They can, however, engage with the leaders of other organisations and hold discussions around areas of capability that may be of interest to all parties. This collaboration is essential at the leadership level.

A capability assessment must be initiated *before* a crisis emerges. This process is key to the leader developing a clear understanding of what their organisation can achieve. It removes assumptions and replaces them with fact. The process is an excellent way of the leader learning about their organisation and then managing the available resources.

Collaboration

Collaboration Within the Organisation

Senior leaders need to be constantly vigilant and objective when receiving briefings from their staff to ensure that capabilities are not inflated either to impress them or to prevent detailed inquiry into areas of capability that are not at an acceptable level. It is a sad fact that some parts of organisations do not always report their levels of capability as accurately as they should. When a crisis strikes, it is too late for the senior leader to find capability gaps. Should an out-of-scale crisis strike, the consequences to communities and economies may be increased because of an unexpectedly poor response.

To gain and maintain an accurate understanding of their organisation's capabilities the senior leader must engage meaningfully with all levels in their organisation. This must be undertaken in the spirit of true collaboration; there should be something to gain for both sides of the discussion. It is not sufficient for a senior leader simply to accept briefings or demonstrations from executives or elements of their organisations without asking penetrating questions when they are building their knowledge of the organisation. Executive briefings or demonstrations can be a solid introduction for a senior leader but the senior leader needs to direct what capabilities need to be examined and how they are to be examined or demonstrated.

Some middle level executives might resent what they see as an intrusion of senior leadership into their areas of responsibility. Making interactions collaborative can ameliorate this response. The senior leader must approach such interactions in the full knowledge that when deficiencies are exposed directly to them there is an expectation that something will be done.

It is most unlikely that every problem identified will be able to be solved immediately by the senior leader. Resource constraints, technology or even legislation may contribute to the identified capability deficiency. The senior leader needs to prepare for such situations with care and develop real empathy with those members of their organisation who are identifying the deficiency. Some deficiencies may not need rectification at all as they may be real but very expensive capabilities that are beyond the scope of an organisation.

Once a deficiency is identified and accepted, it is incumbent on the senior leader to follow up and develop a course of action to rectify the situation. Even if people in an organisation want immediate rectification of a capability deficiency they will generally understand if rectification cannot occur immediately as long as the senior leader presents a credible path forward. This interaction represents a true collaboration and will build trust as long as the plan produced by the senior leader is implemented.

Senior leaders also need to take responsibility and be accountable for the decision that a capability or problem is one that they will not rectify. In these circumstances, the senior leader must clearly state the reasons why rectification will not be sought. They must also state the process that is to be used for the matter to be formally raised again in the future by executives at other levels of the organisation if they feel that it must be revisited.

Collaboration with Other Organisations

Just as collaboration is important within an organisation, collaboration with other organisations is also very important. Understanding the roles and capabilities of different parts of other organisations is essential, especially if it is possible that they may have a role in providing some form of assistance in response to a major crisis.

Organisational capability statements, if they exist, provide a good starting point for building an understanding of the capabilities of another organisation. However, such statements may be out of date or inaccurate. If a senior leader identifies other organisations that may be required to assist in responding to a major crisis it is incumbent on that senior leader to verify that those capabilities exist. It is too late to find out after a request for assistance has been made that a capability has been downgraded, removed or simply never existed.

Senior leaders must, therefore, collaborate with other organisations to verify roles and capabilities. Collaboration should occur at various levels of each organisation and must be part of an action plan initiated by the senior leader. This type of collaboration needs to be actively encouraged and managed. The results of the collaboration should be used to build a knowledge base of how another organisation might be able to assist in a crisis and vice versa.

This necessary collaboration will take time and effort at many organisational levels, hence the need for senior leaders to manage these engagements. The capability picture that is built during these organisational collaborations needs to be analysed and shared.

Organisations that are effective at collaborating and which value such activities highly can be said to possess high levels of *collaborative capital*[2]. In the same way that human capital and financial capital are routinely spoken of and accepted, the concept of collaborative capital needs to be developed and then encouraged by senior leaders.

The building of collaborative capital requires personal time and effort from senior leaders. Busy people can always find compelling reasons why they do not have the time to spend on these activities. Yet they are often the first to express concern when a capability that they think exists does not, in fact, exist. It is imperative that senior leaders work with other organisations to build a shared understanding of what each organisation can do and to identify contact points.

This knowledge then needs to be managed and applied so that it can be used effectively in response to an emerging crisis. Staff members need to be encouraged to get up from their desks and go out and meet members in other relevant organisations and learn what they do and can do.

2   Marot. M., Selsky. J., Hart. W., and Reddy, P. (2005). Research teams in an Australian Biotechnology Field: How Intellectual Property Influences Collaboration. *In Collaborative Capital: Creating Intangible Value (Eds, Beyerlein. M., Beyerlein. S., and Kennedy, F.) Book Series, Advances in Interdisciplinary Studies of Work Teams, Volume 11.*

They need to share their own organisational capabilities. This is not a time-wasting luxury—this is an essential part of doing business. The involvement of senior leaders in this process of building collaborative capital is a strategic activity—it has long-term benefits.

> In 2002 major bushfires were raging around the regional city of Nowra, New South Wales. Assistance was requested and additional firefighters were deployed from other regions in the state. One newly arrived group was given directions to commence back-burning operations at 6.00 am the following morning. At around 10.00 am the next morning the incident controller became aware that the back-burning operation had not commenced as directed. The later start was of no concern to newly arrived firefighters as they believed that ample time was available to complete the task. However, the incident controller was extremely concerned when he realised that the assisting firefighters were only experienced in working in open grasslands and not in dense coastal bush where fire behaviour was very different. The potential for a back-burning operation in dense bush that started late in the morning to become uncontrollable as the day temperature rose was real. Additional resources had to be deployed to ensure that the back-burning operation was contained to the planned area.
>
> A sound understanding of respective organisational capabilities and training was missing.
>
> With more than 20 different firefighting organisations operating in Australia it is important that this understanding is developed. Similar misunderstandings have occurred in many other sectors utilising multi-agency responses.

Formal and Informal Organisations

Knowing how their organisations actually work is critical for senior leaders. Ironically, some senior leaders do not find out that they do not know how their organisation works until they are in a crisis. Organisations have both a formal and an informal structure.

Organisation charts and role descriptions reflect the formal structure and do not necessarily reflect the way an organisation operates on a day-to-day basis—and certainly not in times of crisis. There are relationships and activities that do not follow any lines on an organisational diagram or workflow chart. Some individuals are the 'go to' people in an organisation regardless of their formal position because of past jobs, personality or their 'fit' in the organisation.

Organisational Politics

All organisations have their own internal politics. These are a product of time and the people in the organisation. There will be factions and groups and the 'loners' who do not align with any of the others. The successful senior leader needs both to understand the organisation's internal politics and how to make them work for the organisation so they do not become a disruptive influence.

In the face of a crisis it is essential that the senior leader knows how the various elements can all be brought together rapidly so that maximum energy can be focused on the urgent tasks and that no needless waste of organisational energy is expended on politicking.

> Internal politics has been a feature of firefighting services in Australia for a long time. The Report into the Operational Response to the January 2003 Bushfires in the ACT[3] noted that in the ACT: '...there remains, however, scope for these services to be better integrated. In the Inquiry's view, the next logical step in the evolution of emergency services management in the ACT should now be taken by fully integrating the services' operations.'
>
> Efforts are still being made fourteen years after this crisis to better integrate the activities of these fire services. Legislation has been amended and organisational structures and practices modified. The integration process has been lengthy and is continuing.

3   McLeod, Ron, Inquiry into the Operational Response to the January 2003 Bushfires in the ACT, p206

In 2016 a major dispute surfaced in the Victorian Country Fire Authority (CFA) during the negotiation of a new industrial relations agreement. The heated debate pivoted on how much control the full-time element of the CFA would have over the very large volunteer component of the service. A complete restructure of fire services in Victoria was proposed to break the deadlocked dispute.

In 2018 a similar dispute erupted as firefighters at Tathra, NSW were mopping up after ferocious bushfires devastated the coastal township.

These 'turf battles' drain organisational energy and affect morale. Little progress can be made under these internal political circumstances. Fortunately, fire fighters on the ground appear to be able to ignore this internal politicking and work closely together.

The community is not impressed and their confidence in their emergency services is diminished by these arguments.

Senior leaders must take the time to understand where such turf battles exist and they must be prepared to address them. This does not mean adoption of a hostile and highly adversarial stance is necessary, but rather, the issues need to be discussed and worked through in an open and transparent manner. Politicians need to be prepared to become involved in a non-partisan way; however, this has not always been easy to achieve.

Adequate staff for 24/7 operations

Having sufficient staff to operate 24/7 may be an area that a leader includes in the conduct of their capability assessment. However, it is not unusual to find this addressed as a separate issue as many organisations do not expect to become embroiled in a crisis. But the nature of crises is such that they can, and do, emerge in the most unexpected places.

Business continuity plans typically look to providing a pathway for organisations to continue operation after a major disruptive event, either natural or man-made. Data back-ups, alternate locations and alternate leaders are usually specified and plans developed to transition to a temporary but operative state quickly after the disruption. All leaders need to plan for these situations.

Many crises, however, do not require massive staff relocations, data transfers and the like. Rather, they demand intense effort over what can become quite lengthy periods (e.g. floods, pandemics or the recovery phase of a catastrophic bushfire or tsunami). In these circumstances, additional staff are required to allow response and recovery operations to continue over long periods of time.

The recovery phase of a crisis is always demanding and extended. Also, after the crisis itself has abated there is an urgent need to return to business-as-usual as routine work in many areas may have been stalled while the crisis was at its peak. Recovery centres must operate for months after major bushfires or floods and require a whole-of-government response utilising skilled public and possibly private sector staff. In Australia, several programs now run to provide public servants with the knowledge and skills required to operate in these centres and to deal with very distressed victims of the crisis. These trained staff may be required for extended periods.

Notwithstanding, the provision of the staff for these centres requires planning and funding. The effective leader must factor such requirements into their organisational capability. Regardless of the type of organisation a leader is entering they must consider how they can operate continuously over a 24/7 cycle or how they will operate with reduced staff levels should members of their organisation be required to assist another organisation tasked with managing a crisis.

Adequacy of routine maintenance schedules

Checking that maintenance is being carried out during a capability assessment is important and a leader must do more than a biennial/triennial check that assets are being looked after. The middle of a crisis is hardly the appropriate time to discover that essential maintenance has not been carried out on an asset that is now required to operate at peak performance!

A leader does not need to be an expert in asset maintenance to ensure that everything is being looked after properly. An effective leader can institute a simple system of random checks of various assets to ascertain that resources are being appropriately maintained. Such random checks do not need to be announced ahead of time. Rather, they can be incorporated as a routine part of the leader's visits to parts of their organisation. Simple questions can be asked such as:

- Is the software in use updated to the latest version?
- Are appropriate security safeguards in place on the IT system you are operating and what are they?
- Can I see the service logs of these pieces of mechanical equipment?
- Are any spare parts in short supply?

Short visits and appropriate questions will encourage staff as they can see that the leader is interested in their work and overall resource management in the organisation will improve.

Interoperability and connectivity

If a senior leader can envisage external organisations being called on to help during a crisis it is important that communications and data interconnectivity be considered. If assistance is requested and provided it is essential that organisations can communicate with each other and pass required data between themselves. Issues of interconnectivity need to be identified before a crisis emerges.

Similarly, if assistance is required in the form of equipment, the interoperability of different types of equipment needs to be considered. For example, if additional firefighting assets are sent to assist another jurisdiction they need to be able to communicate with each other, fire hoses need to be able to connect and spare parts exchanged.

In military organisations interoperability between allied forces permeates entire organisational structures. The North Atlantic Treaty Organisation (NATO) has very detailed interoperability standards and these are always considered when new equipment is being acquired by NATO member nations.

NSW Police and NSW Fire and Rescue officers at Rozelle, Sydney after an explosion that killed 3 persons.

An element of interoperability that is often overlooked is that of staff equivalence. When multiple organisations contribute to a crisis response personnel may suddenly be required to work together for the first time. Although these personnel may have similar or even identical position designations, they may have entirely different training and therefore capabilities. A station officer from one fire service may not be capable of performing the same tasks as a station officer from a different state or country. These differences can be ameliorated if common training and assessment exists, but they will never be removed entirely. As a minimum, these differences need to be identified.

These issues must be addressed well before a crisis occurs as there will be no time to rectify the situation if assets from different organisations need to work closely together and find that they cannot do so.

Anticipation

Anticipating a possible need for assistance is a very important element of a successful senior leader's role. This forward thinking takes the senior leader into a strategic role and this should take priority over becoming involved in the detail of the conduct of the initial response to the crisis. Some senior leaders will find this step very hard.

The management of a routine response will often be a comfort zone that the senior leader will naturally gravitate toward. Detailed management of these early responses by senior leaders can be very frustrating and distracting to the junior leaders who have been given the responsibility and training to do the job. They should be allowed to carry out their planned actions with a minimum of senior leader involvement. Notwithstanding, the senior leader should immediately be looking forward to possible requirements.

Out-of-scale events are difficult to comprehend. They are not simple incidents that are responded to, resolved and closed. Major crises consume the entirety of the response capability very quickly and frequently require senior leaders to seek outside assistance in the form of additional resources. This is true of natural disasters, financial/economic disasters and other man-made disasters such as a major military or terrorist attack.

In government areas many arrangements exist for jurisdictions to seek assistance in an emergency from other organisations or other jurisdictions. The same is not necessarily the case in the private sector and this limits the senior leader's response to an internal corporate one when a disaster (for example, a corporate financial crisis) strikes. The pressing decision for any senior leader is, however, when to ask for outside assistance.

If a request for help is made in the early stages of an emerging disaster senior leaders may be accused of over reacting to the event. Political leaders may respond by saying that they are being exposed to public criticism for not providing adequate resources to respond to such an emergency. Some senior leaders may be reluctant to ask for additional assistance because they fear that this is a sign of their own inability to cope with managing a serious event and therefore they are demonstrating weakness.

Anticipating the need for assistance is a skill that all senior leaders need to develop. Seeking assistance at the very time that existing resources are overwhelmed is not a successful strategy. Senior leaders must place themselves in the shoes of those dealing with the response to an emergency and identify what assistance might be useful and when it might be needed.

If, for example, a bushfire may cause very serious losses were it to get out of control, senior leaders should anticipate requests for additional support and be actively engaged in arranging the provision of that support. This may include requesting the pre-positioning of resources close at hand in case they are needed.

In the Australian Capital Territory in May 2004 a bushfire began in the Namadgi National Park after a lone camper failed to extinguish a campfire properly. Strong winds blew embers into dry forest litter igniting a fire that began to spread rapidly. As the weather was cool the fire was not expected to accelerate quickly and a routine response occurred.

When the incident controller arrived at the scene it was reported that the combination of increasingly strong winds and large amounts of fuel meant that the fire had the potential to spread quite rapidly. Firefighting operations commenced.

Senior emergency managers quickly conferred and decided to mobilise earthmoving equipment to a point with rapid access to the fire ground. A worst-case scenario discussion then indicated that, with a relatively small change in wind direction, a nearby rural community in New South Wales would be threatened. This concern led to a request for a firefighting helicopter to be flown in from a Sydney based organisation. The earthmoving equipment was deployed and the helicopter was activated from Sydney. This was all undertaken based on anticipating a possible future need; the incident controller had not requested any assistance at this point.

Two hours after the earthmoving equipment and the helicopter were mobilised the incident controller advised that the wind direction had shifted and that there was a high risk of the fire running toward the rural community in New South Wales. Aerial firefighting support and heavy earthmoving equipment were requested by the incident controller. He was very pleased (and a little surprised) to find that the request could immediately be fulfilled and the firefighting helicopter was in operations against the fire only 15 minutes after the request was made. The earthmoving equipment arrived 30 minutes after the request.

The preparation of this support was undertaken without reference to the incident controller. This is a small but excellent example of how senior leaders provided effective support for front-line personnel by anticipating the need for assistance. In so doing, a possible disaster was averted, as the incident controller could escalate the response and contain and then extinguish the fire without any damage to the rural community that was in the direct path of the fire.

Requesting assistance before it is needed sometimes attracts criticism and accusations of over-reaction. Senior leaders must therefore be prepared to explain the reasons for their actions clearly and the actions taken must be consistent with a reasonable approach to preventing an incident from developing into a major disaster or an out-of-scale event. It is far better to anticipate a possible requirement that does not eventuate than to be confronted with massive losses that could possibly have been avoided.

Asking for assistance is not a sign of weakness but a sign of a leader with their feet firmly on the ground and demonstrating a realistic appreciation of the capabilities of their own organisation. Knowing exactly what an organisation can or cannot do is also an essential prerequisite for being able to frame an out-of-scale event accurately.

Being prepared to ask for additional resources early in the initiation of a major event can allow a degree of control to be exerted that might prevent the event growing into an out-of-scale event. That is, the event is framed in such a manner that makes clear to all concerned that if a major, early response is not commenced an event which may be large but routine, could rapidly grow into an out-of-scale event.

An effective senior leader should always be looking for developments in a crisis that might require the application of different or additional resources. In some instances, readying additional resources before they are needed or relocating assets so they can respond quickly to a future request can mean the difference between success or failure.

Air assets can react quickly when their use has been pre-planned

In almost every case, the early preparation of additional resources will incur a cost. It is therefore obvious that it will not be possible to move or engage extra resources when a crisis has not emerged and the situation reflects business-as-usual. However, a leader can still take very effective steps in anticipation that will save time later if a crisis emerges.

The most effective and cost free anticipatory step a leader can take is to let managers with resources that might be needed in a crisis know that a situation is emerging that could generate a request for assistance. As soon as this information is passed to another element or organisation, information can begin to flow. Preparations can be formulated in leaders' minds and barriers anticipated and perhaps removed in advance. This preparatory work can be done with minimum cost and it will save an enormous amount of time when time is a most critical element.

The action of giving early warning of a possible request for assistance requires a leader to be clear about the capabilities of their own organisation.

Calling for additional assistance when the requested capabilities already exist somewhere in the organisation is a certain way to reduce the amount of cooperation and collaboration with other organisations in the future. Anticipation is therefore effective when the leader has already conducted a thorough capability assessment of their own organisation and as a part of that process, assessed the assistance that other organisations might be able to provide in a crisis.

Requests for additional resources to assist in the response to a crisis may take many forms. However, as soon as the resources of the affected response organisation look like being overwhelmed, and assistance is requested, the response changes in character and becomes much more complex. In addition to dealing with the crisis, issues such as legal requirements, leadership or management responsibilities and accountabilities and sometimes even payment for the assistance, merge into the complexity of the response. It is preferable to anticipate these issues and have such arrangements in place in advance. However, given the nature of catastrophic disasters, this is not always possible.

PART 3
SENIOR LEADERS' BEHAVIOUR DURING A CRISIS

Knowing yourself is the beginning of all wisdom

Aristotle

Chapter 9
Approachability, Sensible Optimism and Calmness

During many lessons learnt projects senior leaders who were not approachable, sensibly optimistic and calm during a crisis response were identified by others as contributing directly to a poor response. This is understandable as who would want to be the bearer of bad news when the recipient is likely to respond angrily and 'shoot the messenger'? If the senior leader expresses pessimism about the chances of controlling the crisis, how can subordinates step up and fill that void without looking cavalier? If the senior leader shouts, uses profanities and slams their hands down on work stations, will others present be able to concentrate on their critical roles in the response?

The answers to each of the three questions above are obvious. The senior leader who does not behave well in the three areas that have been identified can, single-handedly, cause the response to a crisis to falter and even fail.

It is well known that senior leaders need to demonstrate many behaviours to succeed in all the facets of their important role. However, this chapter focuses on approachability, sensible optimism and calmness because these are the key behaviours that a senior leader must demonstrate when their organisation is facing a real crisis.

By addressing all the areas that have been covered so far in this book a senior leader is, in fact, learning how to be approachable, sensibly optimistic and calm when leading a response to a crisis. This technique provides a different development pathway. Learning to lead in the areas covered can be an accelerated personal development process and also an integral component of the senior leader's day to day work.

Approachability

Reflect on the senior leaders that you have admired most. It would be surprising if there were any on your list that were not approachable and did not listen to options that you presented. In a high-pressure situation where you have presented an option to your senior leader and they accepted it, and thanked you for your efforts, how did you feel about the leader? Chances are that you were personally thrilled and that you admired that senior leader's actions. Other members of your team would feel similarly. Because your senior leader accepted your option you would be highly motivated. Your engagement in the efforts to respond to the crisis will increase.

By engaging personally in planning—accurately framing the event, employing strategic thinking and developing situational awareness the senior leader will be much more inclined to engage with others so they can test their thoughts on the emerging situation. Their door is open wide, not slammed shut. By utilising various organisational leadership techniques, the senior leader will not be surprised by unexpected organisational deficiencies. In short, the senior leader will be more confident and positive about their own ability to lead their organisation during a crisis.

With intimate knowledge of the work that underlies the plans that are being implemented and thoroughly understanding that the plan only sets the starting point for the response to a crisis, the senior leader is already disposed to be flexible and agile. Exchanges with other team members regarding developments are then sought by the senior leader.

The understanding of the flexibility that is provided through engagement in the planning process also positions the senior leader to seek good intelligence and information. Resource management becomes a focus on anticipation and response. Collaboration with other organisations becomes an essential and desirable activity.

Sensible Optimism

If a senior leader faces a high-pressure situation with a sense of impending doom and displays pessimism about the chances of responding effectively to the crisis, the rest of their organisation will act in a similar fashion. The reverse is also the case. If the senior leader is very confident in the face of a high-pressure situation generated by a crisis, then other members of the organisation are also likely to adopt a confident and optimistic demeanour. The reality is that the attitude expressed by the senior leader under pressure is rapidly transmitted throughout their entire organisation. Our emotions 'leak' to others and we cannot stop this from occurring.

What is required is sensible optimism. The senior leader must adopt an attitude that demonstrates that they see the dangers ahead but are also aware of the strengths of the organisation that, if properly directed, will allow an effective response to the emerging crisis to be mounted. To be able to behave in this manner the senior leader must have a complete and in-depth understanding of the plans and capabilities of the organisation. Strengths and weaknesses must be understood well in advance of the onset of any crisis.

On 13 January 2011 Brisbane, Queensland was plunged into crisis by massive flooding. The areas surrounding Brisbane had been deluged with rain and the rain, coupled with extensive run-off from land within and around the catchment area of the Wivenhoe Dam, brought the water holding capacity of the dam to dangerously high levels. Dam managers ordered an emergency release of large volumes of water which subsequently contributed to massive flooding of the Brisbane River. The city was stunned and emergency services quickly overwhelmed.

Brisbane Floods 2011

The Premier, Anna Bligh, personally led the immediate recovery efforts and galvanised the residents into action through the use of sensible optimism. She also demonstrated approachability and calmness during the crisis and this lifted the residents to achieve amazing results in the recovery process.

'As we weep for what we have lost, and as we grieve for family and friends and we confront the challenge that is before us, I want us to remember who we are.

We are Queenslanders.

We're the people that they breed tough, north of the border.

We're the ones that they knock down, and we get up again.'

Anna Bligh

The senior leader must, however, be careful not to confuse the adoption of sensibly optimistic behaviour with the development of a 'can do' attitude that might lead to disastrous results. The two behaviours are very different and can have opposite effects on the way in which an organisation responds to crises.

If the senior leader has been thoroughly involved in the key elements of the planning process they will have an excellent understanding of the context that the plan was developed to meet. They will know which factors and limitations have been considered and have a thorough understanding of the options available, regardless of which one was selected as the best option for further refinement.

Knowing that intelligence and information is being managed by competent people and quickly delivered to the senior leader and disseminated to those that need it, builds confidence. If a thorough and up to date capability assessment has been undertaken and collaboration utilised, the senior leader can be sensibly optimistic that a reasonable outcome can be achieved in the response to a crisis.

Some response options may require sacrifices. Damage may be done and it could be serious, as for example, financial losses may be incurred or property lost. But a concerted response by a sensibly optimistic organisation can mitigate those losses and contain the situation.

Calmness

Very few people enjoy working in an environment where there are instructions being shouted everywhere and there is a sense of continual pandemonium. The television and film images of traders on a stock market floor or trading rooms of merchant banks are not the guide that should be followed when dealing with a crisis. The difference between traders in a buying or selling frenzy and the response to a major natural disaster, political policy crisis or other financial calamity is that the traders are responding to the possible outcomes of the crisis as directed by others. They are not planning a collective response to remove the cause of the crisis.

For an effective organisational response to a major crisis, activities must be coordinated and high levels of situational awareness maintained. For these two key ingredients of success to be achieved there must be a sense of calm in the organisation and this begins at the top with the senior leader.

The ability to do this will be greatly improved if the senior leader has ensured that proper plans have been developed to respond to various contingencies and if the senior leader has a thorough understanding of their organisation's capabilities.

If a senior leader has a thorough grasp of strategic thinking and the need for situational awareness, and how to gain it, they are already well positioned to lead calmly. If they combine this knowledge to assist them in framing the event they are unlikely to be totally surprised by adverse developments in the situation. Understanding that out-of-scale events can develop quickly they can be looking for the appropriate signals and even anticipating what would need to be done to respond if such an event developed.

Maintaining a sense of calmness does not mean adopting a casual or complacent approach to the response to a crisis. There is no room for either of these attitudes. The senior leader needs to be personally calm but very clear on the direction in which the organisational response is to head.

By keeping calm the senior leader will also be able to influence others to do the same. The senior leader will quickly become a direct influence on others to remain calm and therefore the work undertaken will be much more effective.

Emotional Intelligence

A study of emotional intelligence (EQ) reveals that people with high levels of EQ are typically approachable, optimistic and calm. The body of knowledge that underpins the concept of EQ is now extensive and has been proven over time. Daniel Goleman, the researcher who first popularised EQ through his outstanding research and excellent books, should be compulsory reading for aspiring senior leaders (see Goleman, Daniel, Working with Emotional Intelligence, Bloomsbury Publishing, London, UK, 1999 and other titles by the same author). Senior leaders who have not yet taken the opportunity to examine EQ and its fundamental importance to success when leading in high pressure situations should learn as much as they can about the subject.

When an EQ diagnostic and subsequent development pathway is undertaken with junior and mid-level leaders some great outcomes can be achieved. However, with senior leaders, the outcomes are often less successful. This is simply because there is insufficient career time left for senior leaders who are not strong in all elements of EQ to develop and practise the competencies that are needed to allow behaviours to change. Additional developmental pathways are required. Learning the practical skills presented in this book provides one such route.

CHAPTER 10
SELECTION AND DEVELOPMENT
OF SENIOR LEADERS

The selection and on-going development of future senior leaders is a logical area for examination at this point. To do so in any detail, however, would shift this book from its focus of being a practical guide for existing senior leaders fulfilling their primary day-to-day role.

It is appropriate however, to flag just a few points for consideration in the selection and development of future senior leaders who require skills in crisis leadership. The brevity of this final chapter is not intended to indicate that selecting and developing future senior leaders is less important than adding to the skills of current senior leaders. It is an area that requires intense effort and a very high priority. The points raised in this chapter are here to stimulate thought about how the contents of this book might be used to change existing processes to ensure that the very best senior leaders are available in the future.

Selecting the Senior Leader

Now that we know how a senior leader should behave during a crisis and the particular skills that will help them act in the desired manner, we can begin to construct meaningful questions that can be used when interviewing a candidate for a position as a senior leader. Each of the skill sets that have been discussed in previous chapters need to be demonstrated by the candidate. If the range of skills is not complete then the interviewing panel should have in mind what action should be taken to fill in the missing elements and how much time this will take.

Questions of general interest such as: 'How do you see this organisation developing in the next five years?' are replaced by: 'How will you ensure that you find enough time to engage in thinking strategically about the challenges this organisation may face over the next five years?' Other questions regarding techniques for framing an event, planning to respond to a crisis, resource management, intelligence and information management and required personal behaviours during a crisis response all replace vague and 'light weight' questions that might currently be used.

If those conducting the selection want to probe more deeply into a candidate's suitability they can undertake a scenario driven assessment. An assessment centre can be set up in which the aspiring senior leader is confronted with a simulated crisis scenario and asked to consider their response at increasing levels of pressure. New technologies such as virtual reality can be used to add realism.

This makes the selection process more relevant, targeted and demanding. Many candidates who have the gift of sounding very convincing in the conventional interview setting may be exposed as wanting during this type of process.

Developing the Senior Leader

All leaders need to have the opportunity to continually develop their personal skills. The proposition being advanced here is that their personal developmental focus should start with the three behavioural areas outlined previously. Working back from these behaviours, development should be targeted towards planning skills and the organisational leadership techniques outlined in Parts 1 & 2 of this book.

Ideally, all of the activities outlined should be occurring routinely in organisations. When the senior leader engages personally in each of these areas, the organisation's potential response to a crisis is markedly improved. Both the senior leader and the organisation are better off.

When the senior leader develops an understanding of the individuals that work in their organisation who are essential for a successful response to a crisis they are in a position to develop them as well. The senior leader comes to understand their personal role in any response and is better able to fulfil it. The attraction of moving back into a former comfort zone diminishes greatly as they now understand what they should be doing and are at ease doing it. They can identify and remove barriers and provide the opportunity for others to do their very best.

More traditional methods of developing EQ competencies can be run for senior leaders if desired. Senior leaders should, however, be ensuring that potential leaders are being identified as early as possible and given an EQ development pathway.

Unfortunately, senior leaders have so much pressure on their time that personal development activities often fall by the wayside. To prevent this occurring, it is suggested that formal development activities should be planned for all senior leaders. Without going into detail, it is suggested that consideration be given to the regular use of the following types of development opportunities for current senior leaders where applicable:

- Virtual reality simulations
- Desk-top simulations
- Formal after-action reviews to determine lessons and procedural changes to ensure that the lessons are actually learnt
- The conduct of inter-jurisdictional exercises to test crisis response plans
- Forums for the improvement of interoperability/interconnectivity standards (in training, procedures and equipment)

The personal development opportunities listed above are already being used by many sectors. However, there are organisations that are not engaged in developing their senior leaders in this on-going way. The increasing frequency of crises means that this is a high risk to those sectors.

CONCLUSION

The last decade in Australia has been one where many crises have occurred. Australia has experienced major drought in some areas and flooding in others. Severe storms have battered coastal communities and intense bushfires have razed entire communities and agricultural areas. The economic cost of these events has been huge.

In the same period, the Australian government has had to deal with major policy failures. These have occurred in areas such as Indigenous policy, energy policy and refugees. Government policies to avert recession through generating policies such as the Home Insulation Program (Pink Batts) became a crisis. Recently, the collapse of the first on-line census to be conducted in Australia was a rude awakening to the challenges of directed cyber-attack.

Globally, the public appetite for failure in the face of a crisis has greatly diminished. The public can generally accept that emergency response measures may not prevent crises from occurring but they will not accept a poor response to a crisis. However, as the public becomes better informed, they are now questioning how effective organisations and their senior leaders are at preventing crises from developing in the first place. Crisis management has become an essential capability in all enterprise areas where once, crisis management was a specialist field typically led by defence and emergency management personnel.

Public information has moved from print media and television with early deadlines and geographically limited reporting coverage to a situation where the news cycle runs 24/7 and provides near real-time, global coverage of events. Add to this the pervasiveness of a variety of social media platforms and the scene is set for citizen reporting to input directly to the mainstream media machine. This change can lift media coverage to real-time reporting such as has been seen with the tsunami in Japan in 2011, hurricanes in the Caribbean, massive wildfires in California in 2017 and the on-going famines in Africa.

Where once the mainstream media were considered reliable sources of information this assumption must now be challenged. Great care must be exercised in selecting sources and deliberate misinformation must be managed.

The work of all senior leaders is now harder than it has been in the past. Traditional methods of preparing personnel to fill these demanding roles need to be reviewed. It would be ideal if all organisations could mirror the training that many defence forces provide for their senior leaders but this is impractical and cost prohibitive. Positive changes can, however, be made.

I believe that it is essential that steps are taken by senior leaders (and those aspiring to those positions) to address the four areas that have been identified as appearing consistently where a response to a crisis has been poor. To reiterate, these four areas are:

- Poor senior leadership skills.
- Poor planning.
- Failure to use information and intelligence effectively.
- Ineffective resource allocation.

Armed with this knowledge, senior leaders can set about ensuring that if they are to improve in any area of their job, they MUST develop high levels of skill in these four areas. All of these skills can be learnt quickly at the basic level and then developed further. The three parts of this book: *Senior Leaders and Planning, Organisational Leadership Techniques and Senior Leaders' Behaviour During a Crisis* attempt to provide a practical basis for overcoming these deficiencies in a senior leader's training and development.

Being able to frame an event effectively is the starting point for crisis response planning. Recognising and understanding how to mitigate the impact of unconscious bias is critical. From here the personal development path should travel through building an understanding of what constitutes strategic thinking and how to improve individual situational awareness.

The so-called 'natural leader' is a person whose brain has software built in from birth that helps them plan in a logical and methodical way. If your brain did not receive that initial software package a simple upgrade is available! By following the steps outlined in Chapters 3 and 4 (Crisis Response Planning and Testing Crisis Response Plans) anyone can improve their skills in this area.

Organisational leadership techniques can be used by senior leaders to focus their actions and build the essential elements of organisational knowledge they need to build their confidence. By using distributed leadership techniques a senior leader can create the mental space to conduct strategic thinking and to focus on important organisational improvement matters. Driving role clarity throughout an organisation has very beneficial results.

As a crisis unfolds it is essential that the senior leader understands what information they need and who is going to sort key elements of that information from the massive amount of inputs that will be received from the moment the crisis begins to develop. Importantly, the senior leader needs to determine what intelligence needs to be disseminated. Having critical intelligence and not ensuring that it is shared with those that need to know is a major cause of failure.

Collaboration within an agency or enterprise is another essential requirement. Organisations need to work as an entity using all available internal expertise and capabilities. By collaborating with external organisations, information and intelligence can be obtained and used. This is essential when dealing with ambiguity when signals are weak. Collaborative capital should be developed and increased just like human and financial capital.

Having resources in the wrong place at the wrong time can be as bad as having no resources at all. The first resource management step a senior leader must take is to understand what capabilities exist in their own organisation. The best way to do this is to conduct a capability assessment. I have worked in areas such as ICT where this has been turned into an art form with highly complex Capability Maturity Models (CMM) being used by technical experts and consulting firms. These audits are helpful but when they are conducted by third parties they may not give a senior leader the necessary close understanding of the capability that actually exists. Senior leaders will benefit by listing the capabilities that they believe should be present in their organisation and then personally requiring business units to demonstrate that these capabilities actually exist.

Once internal capabilities are fully understood the senior leader should look outwards to other organisations that may be able to provide additional capabilities should that be necessary if a crisis emerges. It is not possible to undertake a personal in-depth examination of other organisations but effective collaboration can provide an extensive knowledge base which can then be drawn on during a crisis.

The key to successful application of all of these resources is the ability to anticipate what capability is needed where. Assuming that the senior leader has participated in the planning process prior to the crisis emerging, they will be in a good position to follow changes in the crisis and adapt their response plan accordingly. This will allow the senior leader to anticipate requests for additional resources and to pre-position them if necessary. If resource deficiencies begin to appear then early warning can be given to organisations that might be able to assist with additional capabilities. Anticipation is a key factor in allocating resources in response to a crisis.

The final element is possibly the most important of all—senior leadership behaviours during a crisis. Approachability, sensible optimism and calmness are critical behaviours for an effective senior leader. Ideally, future senior leaders should be identified early in their careers and given the opportunity to develop their personal leadership skills. The best way to do this is to have the potential senior leader undertake an EQ diagnostic and then follow a personal EQ development program. If there are a number of years to practise the required behaviours then it is likely that good outcomes will be achieved.

Frequently, senior leaders have not had this opportunity given to them early enough in their career to allow the personal development process to be followed through to its conclusion. This book has been written as a practical guide to accelerate improvement in these three critical personal behaviours.

If a senior leader can frame an event, think and act strategically, follow a methodical and logical planning process, manage information/ intelligence effectively and understand organisational capability assessment and anticipate resource requirements, they will be much more confident in themselves and their organisations. If they have less anxiety they will be more approachable and calm. If they have benefitted fully from personal involvement in the planning process and if they understand the capabilities at their disposal, they can be sensibly optimistic. In short, they will quickly improve the key senior leadership behaviours that are essential to an effective response to a crisis.

About the Author

Peter Dunn made his first career in the Australian Army. He retired from the Army in 2002 as a Major General after holding many senior leadership positions and being involved in numerous situations that required the use of crisis management techniques. Peter moved to work in the public sector and was subsequently engaged to build and head a new emergency services organisation in the Australian Capital Territory after the disastrous 2003 Canberra bushfires.

After establishing the new organisation, Peter moved into private enterprise where he has operated since 2006. He has worked for major global consulting firms where he specialised in strategic leadership and capacity development. Peter now concentrates his efforts on crisis management and development issues in a global context. He travels widely in remote areas of Australia and internationally.

Peter has extensive experience on both public and private sector Boards. He is currently Chair of the Malpa Institute which works to reduce the social disadvantage being experienced by young Indigenous Australians, particularly in the health sector.

ACKNOWLEDGEMENTS

I wish to acknowledge the support of Noetic Solutions Pty Ltd for my work on this book. Their large data base of lessons learnt projects provided the foundation for my thoughts. The ongoing support of the company has been essential and is appreciated.

Beasley Intercultural has also provided very valuable support by participating in discussions on unconscious bias and leadership behaviours. They willingly shared the company's extensive experience in these areas and they continue to contribute to my thinking.

This book began as a much larger volume. It was going to be a hardcover 'bookend' to years of involvement in the strategic leadership area. However, in one of the many discussions I had with colleagues during the drafting process, they forcefully pointed out that if my work was to be of any use to very busy senior leaders, the product must be brief and to the point. The work was to be for the senior leaders' benefit—not mine! I am very grateful for their advice and, on reflection, I totally agree.

I have come to the conclusion that reducing the size of a draft is much harder than waffling on for pages. As Winston Churchill allegedly once said: 'I would have written you a shorter letter if I had more time.' This quote is very true.

Other colleagues and friends have been pushing me to produce this book. I want to thank them for their persistence and the desire they expressed to see me write this document. Those who have managed crises themselves have generously given their time to review drafts and to input their experiences. We all agree that things can be done better.

I particularly want to thank the hundreds of long suffering participants in Crisis Management and Capacity Development programs that I have run over the years, especially within the Aid and Development sector. It is this group that continues to ask for something more than my program slides as reference material for their ongoing, essential work around the world. I hope this meets their needs.

My editor, Deborah Palmer, has done a wonderful job in helping me produce this book. Thank you for your invaluable advice.

Finally, I must thank the 'critic-in-chief', my wife Lindy, for the critiques and time spent reading drafts and discussing content.

www.ingramcontent.com/pod-product-compliance
Lightning Source LLC
Chambersburg PA
CBHW071600200326
41519CB00021BB/6822